Calvin Goodspeed

Baptism; an Argument and a Reply

Calvin Goodspeed

Baptism; an Argument and a Reply

ISBN/EAN: 9783743313033

Manufactured in Europe, USA, Canada, Australia, Japa

Cover: Foto ©Lupo / pixelio.de

Manufactured and distributed by brebook publishing software (www.brebook.com)

Calvin Goodspeed

Baptism; an Argument and a Reply

BAPTISM:

AN

ARGUMENT

AND A

REPLY.

BY

REV. C. GOODSPEED, A.M.

TORONTO, ONT.

TORONTO
DUDLEY & BURNS, PRINTERS, 11 COLBORNE STREET
1892.

PREFACE.

The first edition of this little work was issued in 1880. Owing chiefly to an over pretentious title for which I was in no way responsible, the balance of the edition left unsold on my return from a year's absence from Canada, was destroyed. A second edition was published in 1882, in reply to Mr. McKay's review of my first pamphlet. This edition has been exhausted. The present pamphlet contains the substance of the preceding one, with some points more fully elaborated and new ones added. Great care has been taken to verify every quotation and to guard every statement. As I seek both to reply to Mr. McKay and carry forward an argument for the Baptist view of the mode and subjects of baptism, the treatment is not as compact as could be wished. Special attention is called to the foot notes and addenda, as they deal with many of the charges and statements of the pamphlet to which mine is an answer. Where it is possible, the reader of this pamphlet should also read those to which I reply, so that he may consider both sides fairly. I can only add a hope that these pages may not be made the occasion for bitterness of feeling by any, but may be of service to the truth, and express a wish for the time to come when candid discussion of disputed points may cause no abatement of the warmth of that Christian fellowship which should exist between all who are followers of the same Lord.

TABLE OF CONTENTS.

Part I.—Mode of Baptism.

Chap.	I.	Introductory...............................	7—12
Chap.	II.	Argument from Classical Usage...............	12—26
Chap.	III.	Argument from Scripture, Objections..........	27—48
Chap.	IV.	" " " Proof for Immersion	48—61
Chap.	V.	" " " " " "	62—68
Chap.	VI.	Argument from Church History..............	68—86
Chap.	VII.	General Summary..........................	86—90

Part II.—Subjects of Baptism.

Chap.	I.	Infants excluded from Baptism of N. Test....	91—102
Chap.	II.	Alleged Old Testament Evidence	103—114
Chap.	III.	The Testimony of History	115—123

BAPTISM:

AN ARGUMENT AND A REPLY.

Chapter I.—General Introduction.

In each of Mr. McKay's successive revisions of his pamphlet, he has retreated from positions attacked in my reviews of his work. He does not, however, in a single instance, confess that his previous statements were indefensible and had to be abandoned. Even where he has maintained, substantially, his former positions, he has, in numerous instances, so changed the form of statement as to make my criticisms unintelligible. A few of the most offensive expressions in the first edition have been eliminated; but enough of them remain to manifest a bitterness of spirit most inconsistent with the sacred work of defending what is esteemed the truth. It had been well had Mr. McKay remembered that his resort to what is fitted to arouse blind prejudice against perhaps the largest denomination on this continent must suggest the suspicion to intelligent minds, that the principles of Baptists cannot be opposed successfully by the nobler weapons of truth. In this review there will be no retaliation in kind, neither will resort be had to the petty arts of small controversialists. One would, indeed, be worthy of gravest censure, if, in dealing with the truth of God, he should forget that he professes to be a Christian and a gentleman, or should be guilty of suppression of facts, perversion of evidence or evasions which may help to lead the unwary astray, but which cannot fail to arouse the divine displeasure.

In common with some others, Mr. McKay would have it appear (p. 8-10) that Baptists, in holding immersion only to be baptism, violate Christian charity. Is not this very puerile? Is the question of what constitutes baptism one of Christian liberty or charity, or one of the interpretation of Scripture? In any case, why should it be thought worse that one act alone should constitute baptism than that it may be any one of these? Besides, Mr. McKay forgets the title of his pamphlet?— " Immersion proved to be not a Scriptural Mode of Baptism but a Romish Invention." The only difference between him and us is this: we admit no baptism to be valid unless according to Scripture, while he accepts as valid baptism that which he brands as a Romish invention. Whether his position or ours is the sounder, the reader must decide.

The age is getting too enlightened, however, to be much longer prejudiced against us by ungenerous references to our Strict Communion, such as Mr. McKay makes. Thoughtful men of every faith see, and candid men of every faith admit, that the principle of Pedobaptist practice at the Lord's Table is fully as strict as ours. They do not receive those whom they esteem unbaptized to the Lord's Table any more than do we. If they thought us unbaptized because immersed, as we them because sprinkled, they would not admit us to the Supper in their churches any more than we them in ours. To remove all doubt here, I quote some representative utterances.

Robert Hall:

"They (Baptists) act precisely on the same principle with all other Christians, who assume it for granted that baptism is an essential preliminary to the reception of the Sacrament. * * * The recollection of this may suffice to rebut the ridicule and silence the clamor of those who condemn Baptists for a proceeding which, were they but to change their opinion on the subject of baptism, their own principles would compel them to adopt."*

---

*Works, vol. III, p. 349.

BAPTISM: AN ARGUMENT AND A REPLY.

Dr. Hibbard, the great Methodist authority on baptism, puts it very tersely:

"It is but just to remark, that in one principle the Baptist and Pedobaptist Churches agree. They both agree in rejecting from communion at the Table of the Lord, and in denying the rights of church fellowship to all who have not been baptized. Valid baptism they (Baptists) consider as essential to constitute visible church membership. This we (Pedobaptists) also hold. The only question, then, that here divides us is 'What is essential to valid baptism?'"*

The (Methodist) *Western Christian Advocate*, June 11th, 1871, says:

"Nor do we doubt that the legitimate order of the sacraments is as our contemporary contends. Baptism very properly comes before the Lord's supper."

Dr. Dick, (Presbyterian):

"An uncircumcised man was not permitted to eat the passover, and an unbaptized man should not be permitted to partake of the Eucharist."†

The American Presbyterian:

"Open communion is an absurdity when it means communion with the unbaptized."

"Let us have unity, indeed, but not at the expense of principle; and let us not ask the Baptist to ignore, or be inconsistent with his own doctrine. Let us not either make an outcry at his close communion, which is but faithfulness to principle, until we are prepared to be open communionists ourselves, from which stupidity may we be forever preserved."

The Interior, another Presbyterian paper:

"We agree with them (Baptists) in saying that unbaptized persons should not partake of the Lord's Supper."

The Independent, when the mouthpiece of Congregationalism:

"We do not see how their (strict Baptist) principle differs from that commonly admitted and established in Presbyterian and Congregational Churches."

These are but samples of testimonies which might be given from Pedobaptist authorities. Further quotation

---

*Baptism, Pt. 2, p. 174.   †Theol. Lect. 92.

of them, however, is not necessary. Every denomination believes that baptism is pre-requisite to membership in the visible church, and that the Lord's Supper is an ordinance of this church. Consistency with these two tenets which are embodied in the creeds of all bodies of Christians binds all to the strict communion practice. No one has a right to church membership if unbaptized: no one has a right to the Lord's Supper unless a church member. It inevitably follows that no unbaptized person has a right to the Lord's Supper. It is to be feared, however, that consistency with their inconsistent outcry against close communion in the Baptist body is impelling some, especially of our Methodist brethren, to disregard the teaching of those who were their leaders in the past and of their standards in the present, and to admit the unbaptized whom they declare outside the visible church to the Lord's Supper which is for those within it.

There is, then, no difference between us and Pedobaptists in the principal which governs our practice at the Lord's table. All the bitter things, therefore, which many Pedobaptists say about Baptist close communion apply in full force to their own denominations.

The attempt to make the reader judge of the tone and spirit of a great denomination by a few harsh expressions culled out of their connection from two or three of its writers will meet with severe reprobation from all fair minded people. More ungenerous invective against Baptists than any Mr. McKay quotes from Baptist writers against Pedobaptists can be found in his own pamphlet. Yet who would judge of the temper of the great Presbyterian body by the tone of his production? The association of Baptists with Cambellites who are most bitterly opposed to them, and with Christadelphians and Mormons merely because these immerse, calls for little reply. Orthodox Pedobaptists might as well be classed with Unitarians and Romanists merely because they all sprinkle candidates for baptism. It needs only be said, as to Mr. Brookman's case, that, as soon as he declared his doubts about the depravity of man, the obligation of the Sabbath and the moral law, etc., to be beliefs, he had to leave our denomination.

Mr. McKay assumes (p. 9) that one cannot be a Christian unless a church member, and that the unbaptized are committed to the "uncovenanted mercies of God," p. 15. This may be Mr. McKay's belief and that of a large proportion of his denomination; but all intelligent people should know by this time, that Baptists hold that a man must become a real Christian through conscious and personal faith on the Lord Jesus Christ before he is qualified for either baptism or church membership, and that we reject with abhorrence the idea that God's covenant mercy is conditioned upon any outward form or relation.

But what shall we say to the statement in the preface of this pamphlet, that Baptists put "the river in place of the cross."* Can any be so ignorant of the prime principle of Baptist belief as not to know we hold that no one has a right to baptism until he has been to the cross for salvation? Do not all know that our protest has been ages long, and often written in blood, against the idea that baptism comes before the cross, and possesses saving efficacy? It is our *peculiar* glory that we have never attached any saving efficacy to mechanical rites, but have viewed them as but signs of a work of grace already done in the heart.†

It will also be news to Baptists that they do not consider baptism a symbol of the Spirit's work in the soul.††

---

*In the last edition of his pamphlet, Mr. McKay modifies this statement, and says, " The error of immersion not infrequently," &c.

†See my Baptist Principles.

††Mr. McKay does not correct this false statement of Baptist belief in the later editions of his pamphlet, but labors through more than a page (pp. 10-11) to stir the prejudices of his readers against us on the ground of this most untruthful charge. He should know that our Pedobaptist friends have really made themselves obvious to the charge of robbing baptism of all necessary symbolism of the Spirit's work in the soul : for they believe it is for babes in whose unconscious souls the Spirit has not begun to work.

All men should know that we think it represents regeneration, by which we die to sin and rise to newness of life.—Rom. 6 : 3-5.

The charges of "garbling" quotations, etc., are most easily made. An opponent can always thus do something to close the minds of his unlearned readers against the force of scholarly authorities which he cannot meet, but must evade. Mr. McKay's charges are all dealt with in their place. I can only say here, that I have been at great pains to verify the quotations in these pages, and will challenge any one to show that I misrepresent a single author I quote.*

We proceed to discuss the question which is to claim chief attention : What is baptism as commanded by our Lord and practised by the apostles ?

Chapter II.—The Mode of Baptism.

1.—CLASSICAL USAGE.

The words "baptize" and "baptism" are transferred from the original Greek in which the New Testament was written. If we can, therefore, find the sense in which these words were used by those who spoke the Greek language, we shall most assuredly know the meaning which they convey in the New Testament; for the Scripture writers would, undoubtedly, use them in their common acceptation. For them to have used them in a different sense from that accepted by their readers, would

---

* Mr. McKay has not ventured to accept this challenge, made in a previous edition of this pamphlet. He indeed says (p. 110) that Prof. Goodspeed represents the Westminster Assembly of Divines as "almost persuaded to be Baptists." I quote their annotation on Rom. 6, 4. If this proves them almost persuaded to be Baptists, then they were almost persuaded, etc., for it is correct. He refers to other alleged Baptist misrepresentations, but I have not used the quotations he speaks of.

have been to court misunderstanding. The only case where there could be an exception to this rule, is that in which there was no word in the language to express the exact meaning to be conveyed. In this case, a word was chosen which was most nearly akin in sense to the desired meaning, and something added to its common acceptation. But, as we shall show further on, there is no instance of such a case in baptism. What then was the

MEANING OF THE GREEK WORD BAPTIZO?

It will save much confusion if we remember that it is only with literal baptism in the material element, water, that we have to do. With its figurative meanings we have no direct concern. Had this been borne in mind, Pedobaptist writers would not have taken the trouble to refer to expressions in Greek writers, in which people are said to have been "baptized in calamity"—"in sleep"—"in taxes"—"by the affairs of life"—"in grief," etc. But even in these figurative uses of the word *baptizo*, we can see the meaning, "immerse," very plainly. "Immersed in calamity," etc., conveys the exact sense, while "sprinkled with calamity," etc., would reduce the sense to nonsense.

What are the facts as to the meaning of literal baptism in water? We have the word *baptizo* frequently in Greek authors, from the earliest times up to, and after, the beginning of the Christian era, and there has not been found an instance of its literal use with water in which it was not an immersion—a burial in water. In view of this fact which can be challenged by no one who dare make any pretension to scholarship, to argue from such figurative expressions as "baptized in sleep"—"in grief"—"in business," etc., that the literal baptism in water of the New Testament was not necessarily an immersion, would be little short of absurdity. As well might we conclude, because English writers use the expressions "buried in sleep"—"in business," etc., that, therefore, the burial of a dead body does not necessarily mean to put it under the ground: but may mean to sprinkle it with earth. And yet, Dr. Dale's great tomes on Classic, Judaic, Patristic and Christian baptism are little else than an attempt to force upon literal baptism in water an imaginary figurative meaning. He gives, as the result of his labors, four meanings to *baptizo*. 1. Intusposition without influence. 2. Intusposition with influence. 3. Intusposition for influence. 4. Influence without intusposition. The last of these meanings is the only one which will help a Pedobaptist to get rid of immersion; but it is a meaning which is the purest figment of the imagination of Dr. Dale, and if it were a meaning, it would get rid of immersion only by making anything which changes the condition of its object its baptism, were it fire, poison, an intoxicant, disease, or what not.

In order to substantiate the statement that literal baptism in water is always an immersion in all Greek literature, we have only to appeal to the testimony of the lexicographers. These laborious scholars carefully study every instance of the use of a word and give the definition which conveys its exact meaning. In every language its lexicographers are the highest authority on the signification of any given word. Now Baptists have challenged anyone to find a single Greek lexicographer who gives as the primary or literal meaning of baptizo anything other than immerse, or its equivalent, and he has not been produced.

I have myself consulted Parkhurst, Stephanus, Maltby, Dunbar and Baker, Jones, Donnegan, Scapula, Skarlatos, Sophocles, Damm, Dunbar, Morell, Hedericus, Schevelius, Liddell and Scott, Robinson, Passow, Schneider, Rost, and they all give immerse as the literal meaning of *baptizo*. I have also before me the definitions of Wright, Leigh, Greenfield, Suidas, Schoettgen, Laing, Bass, T. S. Green, Grove, Stokins, Schwartzius, Mintert, Alstedius, and in n o case is the primary and literal meaning of *baptizo* g iven by any other word than immerse or its equivalent.

When moisten, wet, etc., are mentioned as meanings, it is always as secondary or figurative meanings in which, by a metonomy, the effect of the immersion is put for the immersion itself. Yet our Pedobaptist friends quote these meanings, and do not seem to remember that they have no bearing on the question of the form of baptism, and if they had, that they are against sprinkling. To make this clear, I give a parallel case. Worcester defines the English word "dip," to immerse, to put into any fluid, *to wet, to engage in*. But who would say that the secondary or figurative meanings, *to wet*, and *to engage in*, had anything to do in determining the act of dipping? And yet this is just what some Pedobaptists do in the case of *baptizo*. They refer to its figurative meanings to determine the act of baptism, which is altogether wide of the mark. This is indeed all they ever do in discussing the bearing of the classical use of *baptizo* on the question of the form of baptism.

The history of the definition of *baptizo* in Liddell and Scott's Lexicon speaks volumes. This is the Lexicon which embodies the results of all past research. In the first edition of this great work, "pour upon" was given as a meaning of *baptizo*. Scholars remonstrated. On the most thorough examination, the learned authors found there was no authority for any such meaning, and in the later editions have left it out.

Dr. Charles Anthon, whose classical scholarship was unequalled on this continent, says:

"The primary meaning of the word (baptizo) is to dip or immerse, and its secondary meanings, if it has any, all refer in some way or other to the leading idea. SPRINKLING, etc., are *entirely out of the question*."

Let Dr. Moses Stuart, the celebrated Congregationalist professor, testify as to the Lexicographers generally:

"*Bapto* and *Baptizo* mean to dip, plunge, or immerse into anything liquid. All lexicographers and critics of any note are agreed in this."

And again—

"But enough, 'It is,' says Augusti (Denkw, VII. p. 216), 'a thing made out,' viz., the ancient practice of immersion. So, indeed, all the writers who have thoroughly investigated this subject conclude. I know of no one usage of ancient times which seems to be more clearly made out. I cannot see how it is possible for any candid man who examines this subject to deny this."*

John Calvin:

"It is not the least consequence whether the person baptized is totally immersed, and that once or thrice, or whether he is merely sprinkled by an affusion of water. This should be a matter of choice to the Churches in different regions, though *the word baptize means to immerse, and it is certain that immersion was the practice of the ancient Church.*"†

But how does Mr. McKay, and how do others like him, seek to keep this fact that baptism in all Greek literature meant immerse,—a fact which is indisputable by all who have a reputation for classical scholarship worth sustaining,—from the knowledge of his readers?

Dr. Carson is appealed to as though he was forced to admit that all the lexicographers were against the Baptist view, because he said he had "all the lexicographers

---

* Mr. McKay seeks to make it appear, p. 94, that Baptist writers misrepresent Dr. Stuart's view, and charges upon them, in his own characteristic fashion, the unscrupulousness of the Jesuits. I know of no Baptist writer who uses Dr. S.'s concession of anything else than the classical meaning of *bapto* and *baptizo*. Let him mention a case if he can. In the later editions of his pamphlet, Mr. McKay repeats this charge, although he fails to mention a case, as challenged to do.

† Ins. IV., Ch. 15, Sec. 19, Mr. McKay takes us to task for quoting the sentence in italics, without the context. I did quote the whole passage on another page, I am most happy again to quote it, as it shows how the Presbyterian denomination came to sprinkle rather than immerse in baptism. John Calvin took the liberty to substitute for what he declares the original baptism by immersion, the sprinkling which has prevailed in his denomination ever since. It is thus put by the *Edinburgh Encyclopædia*:—"These Scottish exiles (who had returned from Geneva after the persecution by Mary) who had renounced the authority of the Pope, implicitly acknowledged the authority of Calvin; and returning to their own country, with John Knox at their head, in 1559 established sprinkling in Scotland. From Scotland, this practice made its way into England in the reign of Elizabeth, but was not authorized by the established Church." Art. Bap. See also Ency. Britannica, Art. Bap. Wall's Hist. Inf. Bap. pt. 2, Ch. IX. pp. 461 and 475, etc.

against him in the opinion that *baptizo* always signifies to dip, never expressing anything but mode."*

The facts are these, Dr. Carson in the immediate connection in which these words stand, expressly says, "There is the most complete harmony among them (lexicographers) in representing dip as the primary meaning of *bapto* and *baptizo*," and adds, "Accordingly, Baptist writers have always appealed with the greatest confidence to the Lexicons even of Pedobaptist writers. On the contrary, their opponents often take refuge in a supposed sacred or spiritual use, that they may be screened from the fire of the Lexicons." The exact point at issue between Carson and the lexicographers he illustrates thus: We can say, dip the bread in wine, or moisten the bread in wine. The lexicographers say that because the bread is moistened by dipping, dip means to moisten. Dr. Carson contends that "each of the words has its own peculiar meaning which the other does not possess." So of baptism. Lexicographers, because an object is washed by immersing it in water, give wash as a meaning of *baptizo*. Dr. Carson contends that wash is not a meaning of baptizo, but only the result of the act it describes, under certain circumstances. About the act of baptism there is no controversy between them and Carson: for though they give wash as a meaning of *baptizo*, it is always a washing by immersion in water. Now as the act of baptism is all that concerns us in the ordinance of baptism, we see how much truth there is in the statement that the lexicographers are against the Baptist position, according to the admission of Carson.†

His attempt to show that lexicographers are against us, by direct reference to them, is equally fitted to mislead. He states that certain of them give *baptizo* three meanings—immerse, wash, and cleanse—which is true of

---

* Baptism, p. 55.

† In the face of this explanation, Mr. McKay leaves the old misleading statement in the later editions of his pamphlet.

some of them, but not of all. He then declares, since washing or cleansing can be done in other ways than by immersing an object in the cleansing element, *baptizo* does not always mean to immerse. The false impression which the concealed sophistry of this statement is liable to make cannot be better corrected than by quoting the definitions of some of those to whom he refers.

Schleusner: *Baptizo.* Properly to immerse, and dip in, to immerse in water. * * * *Also, because not unfrequently, something is wont to be immersed and dipped into water that it might be washed, hence it denotes to perform ablution, to wash off, to cleanse in water.**

Scapula: *Baptizo.* To dip, plunge into, plunge under, to overwhelm in water, *wash off, cleanse, as when we im-*

---

* Mr. McKay seeks to make capital out of the fact that I omitted a part from Schleusner's definition. I omitted what had no bearing on the point under consideration, as is always done. I am glad, however, that reference has been made to this matter, as it gives an opportunity to correct a false impression, viz.: that Schleusner declares *baptizo* never means immerse in New Testament usage. His full definition is:

"*Baptizo.* Properly, to immerse and dip in, to immerse in water, from *bapto*, and corresponds to the Hebrew *taval*, 2 Kin. 5: 14, in the Alex. Version, and to *tava* in Sammachus, Ps. 68: 5, and in an unknown writer in Ps. 9: 6. In this signification it is never used in the New Testament, but frequently in Greek writers, for example, V. c. Diod. Sic. 1. c. 36, concerning the overflow of the Nile. Many land animals, overtaken by the river, perished by the submersion."

"In this signification" refers to the signification of *tava*, immediately preceding, viz.: to destroy by immersion. In such a signification as this, it is not found in the New Testament, but often in Greek writers, of which the case given is an instance.

That this must be Schleusner's meaning, and not that baptism in the New Testament is never an immersion of any kind, is plain from his definition of *Baptisma.* Here it is:

"*Baptisma* is a verbal noun from the perfect passive of the verb *baptizo.* 1. Properly, immersion, a dipping into water, a bathing. Hence it is transferred. 2. To the sacred rite which, pre-eminently, is called baptism, and in which formerly they were immersed in water, that they might be obligated to the true divine religion."

Here he declares that New Testament baptism was an immersion. He was too great a scholar to deny this on the same page in his definition of *baptizo.* So much for this "exposure."

merse anything in water for the sake of coloring or washing it.

Parkhurst: *Baptizo.* 1. Dip, immerse, or plunge in water. 2. Mid. and Pass. To wash one's self, be washed, washed, *i.e., the hands by immersing or dipping in water.* The 70 use bapizomai. Mid. *for washing one's self by immersion.*

Alstedius: " To immerse, *and not to wash except by consequence.*"

Schwarzius: " To baptize, to immerse, etc., *to wash by immersion.*" Luke 11 : 38. Mar. 7 : 4.

Mintert : " To baptize : properly, indeed, it signifies to plunge, to immerse, etc. ; *but because it is common to plunge or dip a thing that it may be washed, hence it signifies to wash.*"

The lexicographers then say—such as explain the meaning wash—that *baptizo* means to wash, only as the washing is by immersion. Mr. McKay, and other controversialists of his type, quietly assume, because baptism is sometimes a washing, that a washing is always a baptism however done. So they talk of a floor being washed by water poured upon it, etc., and say here is a baptism which is not an immersion. The reasoning put into a syllogism is : to baptize is to wash, to pour is to wash, therefore to baptize is to pour. The transparent fallacy of this can be seen by a parallel case. To burn is to destroy, to drown is to destroy, therefore to burn is to drown. What cannot be proved, if such is to go for argument.

There is an attempt made on p. 18, to make it appear that baptize cannot always mean to immerse, because the Baptist. Dr. Conant, in his *"Baptizein"* takes seven words to express its meaning in the various cases of its use. Has Mr. McKay never heard of synonymous words ? Had he given the words used by Dr. C., viz., dip, immerse, immerge, submerge, plunge, imbathe, whelm, and stated that the two last are meanings of the figurative use of *baptizo,* any reader would have seen that they all convey the one meaning of covering in an element, which is all that the Baptist position demands.*

Mr. McK. accepts the statement of Mr. Gallaher, that "excellent classical scholar," that "in every instance" quoted by Dr. Conant before the time of Christ, "the baptizing element or instrumentality is moved and put upon the person or thing baptized, never is the person put into the element." The "classical scholarship" displayed in this statement can be judged of by reference to the two following cases, two of many referred to. Ex. 6, "And even if the spear falls into the sea, it is not lost: for it is compacted of both oak and pine, so that when the oaken part is immersed (baptized) by the weight," etc. Ex. 61. "The water solidifies so readily around every-

---

*In his revised edition, p. 102, Mr. McKay states that Dr. Conant "does not undertake to give the ground idea common to" these seven words, and adds, further on :—" Dr. Conant says, *baptizo* does not mean just and only to dip, nor to plunge, nor to immerse. I cannot say, in a word, what it does just and only mean, but it means the ground idea common to dip, and plunge, and immerse, and immerge, and submerge, and imbathe, and whelm. Now what that is I cannot find any word to tell. All the help I can give you is to say : to be baptized is not just to be dipped, nor just to be plunged, nor just to be immersed, but it is just to get the ground idea common to those seven words I have mentioned, and I can only say, the nearest that comes to the meaning, in my opinion, is--im-merse." Now this is meant. I suppose, for wit. However this may be, it is not true. What Mr. McKay says Dr. Conant "does not undertake" to do, this great scholar does in the sentence introducing the one which Mr. McKay quotes (*Baptizein* p. 87) in these words : "From the preceeding examples it appears that the ground idea expressed by this word—baptizo—is to put into or under water (or other penetrable substance), so as entirely to immerse or submerge." It seems incredible that Mr. McKay could have failed to read the one of the two sentences of the paragraph of which he quotes the other. If he did read this sentence, how could he make this point blank denial of what that sentence asserts? His attempt (pp. 102 and 103) to show that Baptists are not agreed as to the meaning of *baptizo,* because different Baptists give, as its signification, dip, plunge, immerse, cover in an element, shows sapience worthy of the author of Mr. McK's pamphlet, and deserves all the reply I herewith give it.

thing that is immersed (baptized) into it, that they draw up salt crowns, when they let down a circle of rushes."*

Mr. McKay, p. 19, refers to a few instances, quoted from Dr. Dale, to show that baptism does not mean " to dip," in the sense of putting in a liquid and taking out again He and others, assume that Carson used dip in this sense, and so they give passages where *baptizo* means only to put under, and then speak triumphantly as though they had demolished the Baptist position. Dip, in the sense of both putting into, and taking out again, is unusual. Worcester in his smaller lexicon gives no such sense. He defines it to immerge, to put into any fluid." It is in this sense that Dr. Carson uses it as a definition of *baptizo*. Dr. Conant gives the meaning of the word thus, " The word immerse, as well as its synonyms immerge, etc., express the full import of the Greek word *baptizein*. The idea of emersion is not included in the meaning of the Greek word. It means simply to put into or under water (or other substance) without determining whether the object immerse sinks to the bottom, or floats in the liquid, or is immediately taken out. This is determined, not by the word itself, but by the nature of the case, and by the design of the act in each particular case. A living being, put under water without intending to drown him, is of course to be immediately withdrawn from it; and this is to be understood wherever the word is used with reference to such a case." From this quotation it can be seen how correct is Mr. McKay's statement, p. 100, that my definition of

---

* Baptizein, pp. 88 and 89.

In my first pamphlet I overlooked the clause "before the time of Christ" as qualifying Mr. Gallaher's statement, and quoted instances after our Lord's time. Because of this inadvertence, Mr. McK. charged me with **intentional** falsification. In my reply, I quoted the instances given above, which are "before the time of Christ," as are many others of a similar kind, thus proving my previous error to have been due to a mere oversight. Mr. McKay has elected to let the old accusation stand, and thus is himself guilty of the exact wrong he so recklessly charged upon me.

baptism as "a covering of a person in water," is "original," and p. 102, that to give "the ground idea" of the various uses of *baptizo* is "what Dr Conant does not undertake to do." It is a little amusing, however, to be told that (p.18) Dr. Conant has been compelled to acknowledge that the Greek word *baptizo* does not mean "the taking out of the water," through Dr. Dale's Classic Baptism, when Dr. Conant's work was published first, and Dr. Dale uses Dr. Conant's original researches at second-hand in the composition of his Classic Baptism.

Thus we have followed Mr. McKay, as he has made these attempts to overturn all the Greek Lexicons, and show that, what the scholarship of the age admits without question, that the literal meaning of *baptizo* is to immerse, is a mistake. It is not every man who would venture upon such an attempt, but it is not always that the less instructed are the most prudent. Until at least one case of literal baptism can be found in classical usage which is other than an immersion, we can well afford to smile at such attempts as the above. The only purpose which can be served by them is to confuse and mislead those who have no independent means of knowing the truth.

But what if it might be shown that in one or two cases out of hundreds *baptizo* did mean something else than immerse, would the Scripture writers, as they wrote the word for the people, have used it in this extraordinary sense which must have been unknown to the people generally, or in the sense in which they were accustomed to use it? Happily, there is not even this possibility of confusion, since no one instance can be found where it does not convey the meaning of immerse. We have its use by men who lived in our Lord's time, and in the time immediately preceding and succeeding,—by Strabo, Plutarch, Diodorus Siculus, Epictetus, Demetrius, and in all their references it is an immersion and nothing else. We have its use very frequently by Josephus, a fellow-countryman and contemporary of the apostles, and writing in the Hellenistic Greek used by them. The following cases will show how he used it, and how the people of Palestine would understand it:

"Continually pressing down and immersing (baptizing) him while swimming, as if in sport, they did not desist till they had entirely suffocated him."*

"And there, according to command, being immersed (baptized) by the Gauls in a swimming bath, he dies."†

"As I also account a pilot most cowardly who, through dread of a storm, before the blast came, voluntarily submerged (baptized) the vessel."‡

Now if sprinkling or pouring were the apostolic form of baptism, we have to suppose the Scripture writers chose *baptizo* to express an act which the people knew it had never meant, while they pass by the words *rantizo* and *cheo* which always expressed these very acts.

It is not enough for those who hold that sprinkling was the Scriptural baptism to attempt to show that *baptizo* does not always mean to immerse. They must prove that its usual meaning, at least, was to sprinkle. But this as a meaning of *baptizo*, as Dr. Anthon in the quotation on p. 15 well says, is "*out of the question.*" There is no way, therefore, to believe that the apostles used *baptizo* to enjoin the rite of sprinkling, unless we suppose they used a word which they knew the people understood to mean immerse and never to sprinkle, to enjoin sprinkling, while they ignored the word *rantizo* which they knew the people understood as expressing this very sprinkling. Those who can believe the Scripture writers guilty of such folly can hold to sprinkling if they will. I cannot believe this of them, and so I cannot believe that sprinkling or anything but immersion, which the word invariably meant, was the baptism of the apostolic day.

*Jewish Antiquities, Bk. XV., Ch. 3, 3. †Jewish War, Bk. 1, Ch. 22, 2. ‡Jewish War, Bk LII, 8, 5.

But some, as does Mr. McKay, hide behind a supposed sacred use "to screen themselves from the fire of the lexicons."

But this is vain.

Baptism in water is a definite act. The word to describe this act for a common purpose would serve equally well to describe it for a sacred one. Thus it was in the Old Testament, sprinklings and bathings of the law. The words used to describe the sacred sprinklings and bathings, were the words in common use to describe these acts for ordinary purposes. No word takes on a new meaning in the Bible to express a religious idea, unless there be no word already in use with that meaning. This is so in accord with fact and common sense that it needs no proof. Why give to a word a meaning it never had, in order to have two words to mean the same thing? There were no lack of words in the Greek to express every meaning which baptism has been supposed to signify. If it was a sprinkling, there was *rantizo*; if a pouring, *cheo*; if a purification, irrespective of mode, *katharizo*. Why then give a word which never meant anything but immerse, either of these meanings in its sacred use, and ignore the words the people all knew conveyed these very meanings? This would be to court confusion and misapprehension. The figment of a sacred use, in such a case as this, is the desperate resort of a lost cause.

ADDENDA.—In his first pamphlet, Mr. McKay gave a list purporting to be cases of the use of *baptizo*. In my review I showed that the most of these were instances of the use of *bapto*, a word never used of the Christian ordinance. This list has been omitted in the later editions.

I find that Mr. Lathern, Baptisma, p. 137, sq., gives a list of definitions, etc., purporting to be meanings of baptize. He indeed remarks that the author from whom he quotes does not sufficiently discriminate between the verbs *bapto* and *baptizo*. But the ordinary reader would not imagine that every meaning there given which is inconsistent with immerse, is of *bapto* and not of *baptizo*.

BAPTISM: AN ARGUMENT AND A REPLY. 25

The quotations on pp. 140, 141, are all, with two, perhaps three exceptions, of the use of *bapto*, and have no bearing on the question of the form of Christian baptism.

In his second and revised edition of his pamphlet, Mr. McKay offered to give $100 to any Baptist who will produce any lexicon of first-class authority, that gives "dip," "plunge," or immerse as the meaning of *baptizo* in the New Testament. In my reply I called this harmless bravado, and added :—" He knows that the lexicons generally give baptize as the meaning of *baptizo* in the New Testament, transferring the Greek word, as does our Bible, and not defining it." I can refer him, however, to Cremer, Biblico Theol. **Lex. N. Test.** Greek, who says, "The peculiar N. T. and Christian use of the word (*baptizo*) to denote immersion, submersion for a religious purpose—to baptize, may be pretty clearly traced back to the Levitical washings"—to Sophocles, who, after defining the classical usage as to dip, immerse, sink, **declares** " There is no evidence that Luke and Paul and the other writers of the New Testament put upon this verb meanings not recognized by the Greeks "—to Wahl's Clavis of N. Test. (1829) which says *baptizo* is used " properly and truly concerning sacred immersion."

I can also refer him to definitions of the noun *baptisma*, baptism.

Liddell and Scott, I. "That which is dipped. II.—foregoing N. Test."

Schleusner. See p. 18.

Stokins, "Generally and by force of the original, it denotes immersion or dipping. 2. Specially, a, Properly, it denotes the immersion or dipping of a thing in water that it may be cleansed or washed. Hence it is transferred to designate the first sacrament of the N. Test. . . . in which those to be baptized were formerly immersed into water : though at this time the water is only sprinkled upon them," etc.

Will this do as answer to this bravado ?

In his last editions, he has withdrawn the challenge.

To the above, we will add the testimony of Thayer's translation of Grimm's Lexicon of New Testament Greek, recognized by the scholarship of the world as the most authoritative work of the kind ever published.

Baptizo. In the New Test. it was used particularly of the rite of sacred ablution, first instituted by John the Baptist, afterwards by Christ's command, received by Christians, and adjusted to the nature and constitution of their religion, viz. :—an immersion in water performed as a sign of the removal of sin.

Baptisma. A word peculiar to New Test. and ecclesiastical writers, immersion, submersion.

His question, p. 24, why, if *baptizo* means immerse, the early Latin Versions do not translate it by *immergo*, and not transfer it, does not require a "Baptist scholar" to answer. Why should these Versions translate rather than transfer the word *baptizo*, if it meant immerse, any more than if it meant sprinkle, or anything else?

To the declaration in his first revised edition, that "all translations of the Scriptures in all languages ever since, with the exception of the recent Baptist sectarian version, which was still-born, have followed the example of the early Latin translation, and transferred, without translating *baptizo*," we replied: this statement must have been made purely at a venture. Dr. Conant, in *Baptizein*, mentions the Syriac (2nd cent.), Coptic (3rd), Ethiopic (4th), Gothic (4th), Lower Saxon (1470-80), Augsburg (1473-75), Luther's (1522), Dutch (1526), Swedish (1526), Danish (1605), which not only translate *baptizo*, but translate it immerse. To this list might be added many others.

In his last revised edition, he evades the force of this criticism by declaring that "*nearly* all," etc.

Mr. McKay refers to my explanation of the baptism *epi koite* (Clem. Alex. Stro. B. 4, Ch. 22, Sec. 144), and impugns my scholarship, because I do not accept his translation.—"This is a custom of the Jews, in like manner also to be often baptized upon the couch," p. 112. Now the learned translators of the Ante Nicene Library translate this passage, "It was a custom of the Jews to wash (baptize) frequently *after being in bed.*" Perhaps my scholarship does not suffer more by agreeing with them against Mr McKay than does his in being against them and with himself.

I quoted Dr. Dale, in my first pamphlet, as follows: "An object baptized is completely invested in the baptizing element," and referred it to p. 129 of his Clonic Baptist. Mr. McKay taxed me with misrepresenting Dr. Dale, because no such words were found on p. 129. I find that the quotation is from p. 127. On p. 31 Dr. D. gives, as the primary meaning of *baptizo*, the following: "*Baptizo* in primary use, expresses condition characterized by complete interposition (being placed within) without expressing, and with absolute indifference to the form of the act by which such interposition may be affected, as also without other limitation —TO MERSE." It is only by using the supposed secondary meaning of *baptizo*, which expresses result and not act, to describe Christian baptism which is an act, that Dr. Dale denies this rite should always be a *mersion*, according to his own definition.

Chapter III.—The Argument from Scripture.

GENERAL CRITICISM.

Mr. McKay says, p. 23, "Presbyterians or any others do not hold that baptize means to sprinkle any more than it means to dip or immerse. They believe that it always expresses *a condition or result irrespective of the mode or act by which it is brought about*, and that in Scripture it denotes a thorough change of spiritual condition effected by the Holy Ghost applying the blood of sprinkling to the soul. And this spiritual baptism of the soul is made manifest or signified by an external rite in which pure water is sprinkled or poured upon the person. But in all this, the word baptize has no reference to mode." As he, in common with a certain class of Pedobaptist controversialists, has adopted Dr. Dale's strange notion, let us examine this statement which embodies the view for which he contends.

1. According to all the lexicographers, so far as they express themselves, the literal meaning of *baptizo* is an act, and a result only as a consequence. Dr. Dale then takes issue with all these. Because, however, baptism, like all other acts, must have an effect in changing the condition of its object, he defines baptism generally as a change of condition. Because the definite act of baptism which Dr. Dale admits is, as he prefers to describe it, a mersion, results in changing the condition of its object, he argues that any change of condition, effected by any act, however dissimilar to this it may be, is baptism. In this way the meaning of baptism as a definite act is gotten rid of, and the result of the act, without reference to the way in which it is brought about is said to be the baptism. In the Christian ordinance, therefore, the act has nothing to do with the baptism, which is purely a change of condition.

Let us try Dr. Dale's process upon some other word —to burn, for instance. One of the results or changes of condition effected by burning is to take away life. Taking away life, then, however effected, is to burn, according to this legerdemain of Dr. Dale. Therefore, to take away life, be it by freezing, drowning, starving, etc., is to burn, equally with consuming in the fire. Yet this attempt of Dr. Dale, which has been the quiet amusement of all scholars who do not wish to make much of it for controversial purposes, is supposed to have demolished the Baptist position!!!

Remembering that a definition is to distinguish the meaning of one word from that of all others, the absurdity of this as a *definition* of baptize is evident to a child. For do not all active verbs change the condition of their objects, or produce results? and do not all verbs in the passive, and some in the neuter express condition? To burn, to freeze, to devour, to destroy, to drown, to build, to strike, etc., and a host of others must then mean to baptize: for they all express a condition or result. Dr. Dale is to be commended for his patient industry. But to give to a word a meaning so general as to apply equally well to hundreds of others, in order to define or distinguish it from all others, is transparent folly.

2. Mr. McKay's definition (?) of baptism quoted above, like that of his master, Dr. Dale, leaves no place for water baptism. Scriptural baptism is "a change of spiritual condition effected by the Holy Ghost." No outward rite in water either is, or effects "a change of spiritual condition." Besides, Mr. McKay adds that this change of spiritual condition, which alone is Scriptural baptism, is "effected by the Holy Ghost," and not by any rite performed by men. And yet, he makes this statement with the N. Testament in his hands, wherein our Lord commanded his followers to baptize believers in the name of the Father, Son and Holy Spirit. He declares that baptism is alone effected by the Holy

Ghost, in the face of the command of Christ to men to baptize, and in face of any number of instances in which men are declared to have baptized others. And does he not, and do not Pedobaptists generally, call the outward rite a baptism? How it is possible for anyone to flatly contradict the N. Testament and deny their own common use of language, in order to attempt to attack immersion and evade attack upon sprinkling by hiding behind a mist, we cannot understand. One question is sufficient to sweep away all this confusion of ideas It is this. If the word *baptizo* has nothing to do with mode or act, but always signifies condition or result, why was it used by inspired men and by our Lord to describe water baptism, which is an act, and not result or condition?

3. But Mr. McKay explains, p. 25, "But although the word *baptizo* does not indicate *mode*, and therefore cannot indicate the specific act of sprinkling any more than it indicates the specific act of dipping, yet as the water baptism is an outward and visible sign of an inward and spiritual cleansing, that mode will be most scriptural and appropriate which corresponds most fully with the mode in which that inward cleansing is represented as taking place."

Who can now fail to understand? The word *baptizo* does not indicate mode, and the Scriptural baptism—a change of condition effected by the Holy Ghost—has no mode. This latter, nevertheless, has "a mode in which it is represented as taking place," and this is a sprinkling. There is a water baptism, after all, although the water baptism is not, and does not effect the change of spiritual condition, which only is Scriptural baptism; and this water baptism, which is therefore not Scriptural baptism, has a mode—sprinkling—to correspond to the "mode in which the real baptism is represented as taking place." To describe this definite modal act of sprinkling, our Lord uses the word *baptizo*, which never indicates mode in its N. Testament use. How admirably lucid!!

Try as he may to conceal it, according to Mr. McKay's statements, *baptizo*, which he declares expresses "a condition or result," and not mode or form of action, is said to be used by our Lord to describe sprinkling or pouring, which express action or mode, and not result. All the lexicographers and even Dr. Dale, declare that *baptizo*, in its primary meaning referring to a definite act, means immerse, or merse, as Dr. Dale prefers. They all declare that this word never means to sprinkle or to pour. Greek literature has been searched through and no case has been found which can be tortured into such a signification. And yet, Mr. McKay would have his readers believe that this word *baptizo*, which always meant immerse or its equivalent when referring to a definite act, is used by our Lord to describe the definite act of sprinkling or pouring. He would attribute to our Lord more tremendous folly even than this. He would have us believe that he passed by the Greek words *rantizo* and *cheo*, which meant the definite acts of sprinkling and pouring he wished to enforce upon the people, and chose a word which never meant this, but always meant another definite act. It is worse than vain to attempt to rule out immerse as a meaning of *baptizo*, on the ground that the word means condition or result and not act, and, at the same time, hold that it was used by our Lord and his apostles to designate as definite an act—to sprinkle.

4. How simple the whole matter is when we accept the facts. Baptism in water is to represent "a thorough change of spiritual condition effected by the Holy Ghost." In this we heartily agree with our opponent. It is to symbolize regeneration, John iii. 5; the complete cleansing effected by regeneration, Acts xxii. 16; Titus iii. 5; change of nature in regeneration by which we die to sin and arise to newness of life, Romans vi. 3 6; Col. ii. 12. This death to sin and resurrection to newness of life—this complete cleansing, is adequately symbolized by burial in water which represents both death and com-

plete purification at once, and so is fitted to its purpose of declaring that complete change by which old things pass away and all things become new. This specific act, so symbolical of this inner change, is signified by the word used by our Lord to describe and enjoin it, as we find by reference to its use by writers and lexicographers. Thus all is consistent—no obscurity, no difficulty; while on Mr. McKay's assumption, everything is misty, inexplicable, contradictory.

5. But in Heb. x. 22, we have an authoritative declaration of Scripture which should give an everlasting quietus to the specious idea that the water baptism must conform to the representation of the mode in which the work of the Spirit is said to be performed, and not rather represent the effect of this inner work on the soul. "HAVING THE HEART SPRINKLED FROM AN EVIL CONSCIENCE, AND THE BODY WASHED IN PURE WATER," says the Scripture. *The outward symbol is to represent the effect of the Spirit's work on the heart, and not to conform to the representation of its mode. The latter is sometimes a sprinkling, the former is a washing.**

Let us proceed to notice the

---

* This one almost self-evident fact that baptism is the symbol of the Spirit's work in us—not of the figurative representation of the mode of the Spirit's work upon us—that in baptism we profess and declare what the Spirit has effected in our hearts, not the way in which the effect is said to have been produced, is a sufficient answer to the greater part of "Baptisma," by Rev. J. Lathern, and to not a little of Mr. McKay's pamphlet. Mr. Lathern's chief reliance is upon the statement, repeated again and again, that as in the Old Testament it is said, "So shall he sprinkle many nations," etc., and that as in the New the Spirit is said to be "poured out," therefore baptism is a sprinkling or pouring. He seems also never to have noticed that the prophets of the Old Testament speak of the Saviour's work as a washing, Is. iv. 4, Ps. xxvi. 6, li. 2-7, Jer. iv. 14, as a fountain of cleansing, Zach. xiii. 1, and represent it by other figures. If then baptism must be a sprinkling to conform to the figurative representation of the Saviour's and Spirit's work as a sprinkling, it must be a washing or bathing to conform to the representation of that work as a washing or bathing, and so of all the other figurative representations. Besides, baptism, in the New Testament is called a burial, to represent the death to sin, and it is called a washing, to represent the complete purification of the regenerate life, Rom.

INSTANCES OF BAPTISM IN THE BIBLE WHICH ARE SUPPOSED TO FAVOR SPRINKLING.

And first, let us examine the alleged argument for sprinkling from the DIVERS WASHINGS (BAPTISMS) of Heb. ix. 10.

In these Mr. McKay sees nothing but sprinkling. He assumes that the apostle identifies the sprinklings mentioned in vs. 13, 19, 21, with these "divers baptisms" of v. 10. The apostle does no such thing, as any reader can see for himself. Had he intended to refer to these sprinklings of vs. 13, 19, 21, in v. 10, he would have said "divers *sprinklings*," and not baptisms, for baptism never in all literature ever meant to sprinkle. He next quotes Lev. xix. 13-20, and Heb. ix. 13, to show that the essence of purification was in the sprinkling, and then asserts that "God's word says that the sprinkling constituted the baptism." The most that these passages prove is that, in the cases specified, sprinkling was necessary to the purification. But it does not say that nothing else was essential to even these purifications, much less that there were no purifications except by sprinkling, which is needed to justify Mr. McKay's statement. The fact is there are ten purifications by bathing in the Old Testament to one by sprinkling, and purification by unmixed water in the Old Testament was *always* by bathing, *never* by sprinkling. Mr. McKay's bluster, in the sentence "it is worse than quibbling for Baptists to say, that in connection with the sprinkling there was a bathing, and that this constitutes the baptism," will not count for much under these circumstances. To establish his conclusion that the "divers baptisms" of Heb. ix. 10 were sprinklings, he assumes that nothing but sprinkling was

---

vi. 3-5, Acts xxii. 16. *It is never called a sprinkling.* Why then should we ignore these representations of the results of the Spirit's work on the heart, which baptism is declared to symbolize, and insist that baptism must conform to the figurative representation of the mode of that operation, which the Scripture never says is to be symbolized in baptism? We wonder that men even urge such an argument.

a purification in the Old Testament, and that these baptisms were purifications and therefore sprinklings. The first of these premises is utterly false.

But as this passage is much used by a certain class of controversialists, and their remarks are fitted to confuse, we propose to give it a thorough examination.

Let us first examine Heb. ix. 10, to find its real meaning.

First: the "divers baptisms" are called carnal ordinances; for the word "and" of the clause "divers baptisms and carnal ordinances" is without MS. authority, and is omitted in the Revised Version. Thus the "divers baptisms" are restricted to such rites as pertain to men's bodies; for "carnal" means "of the flesh."

Second: the ordinances here referred to were to continue until the "time of reformation," viz., until Christ should come.

No rite then which did not refer to outward physical cleansing, and which did not continue to be observed until Christ came, can be referred to by the "divers baptisms."

Bearing these two facts in mind, let us turn to the Old Testament and question it as to the forms of personal purification among the Jews. There are five cases of the sprinkling of men's bodies. At the ratification of the covenant, Ex. xxiv. 18—at the consecration of Aaron and his sons, Ex. xxix. 21, Lev. viii. 30—at the consecration of the Levites, Num. viii. 7—at the cleansing of lepers, Lev xiv. 7—at the cleansing of those defiled by contact with death, Num. xix. 13-21. But the sprinkling of blood at the ratification of the covenant was never repeated. Neither was that of ashes and water at the consecration of the Levites: for it was a consecration of the whole tribe, once for all. Neither, probably, was that of the priestly caste: for it was of the whole priestly class, through their heads.* These sprinklings then

---

* Smith's Bib. Dic. Art. Priest.

could not have been referred to in the divers baptisms: for they were not to continue "until the times of reformation." Only two sprinklings remain, then, which could possibly be referred to, and one of these—that of the leper—did not occur, probaby, once in a generation, if it did so often; for it was next to a miracle for a leper to be cured, and the rite was not to cure lepers, but to celebrate their healing. There was really, then, but one sprinkling of any frequency of recurrence to which these baptisms *could* refer. Is it probable that the apostle applied the term "divers" to the sprinklings of the old economy, when there were but two cases to which he could refer, and one of these so infrequent as to scarcely deserve notice? So much for the probability that the "divers baptisms" refer to sprinklings, apart from the inherent improbability that the apostle would call sprinklings baptisms, when baptism never meant to sprinkle.

But were there any other purifications of men's bodies to which they might refer? Yes, verily, although those who seek to have the reader see sprinkling in the "divers baptisms" do not seem to have considered them. There are forty specified cases where the clothes are to be washed. As the cleanness of the clothes has to do with that of the body, these cases come legitimately under the head of carnal ordinances. But apart from these, there are thirty cases where the whole body of individuals is to be bathed or washed. So much care has been taken to conceal these facts, that we give the most of the passages that the reader may consult them for himself.

Washing of clothes, Lev. xi. 25, 28, 40; xiii. 6, 34, 54 xiv. 8, 9, 47, xv. 5, 6, 7, 8, 10, 11, 13, 21, 22, 27; xvi. 26, 28; xix. 16. Num. viii. 7, xix. 7, 10, 19; xxxi. 24.

Washing of the whole body, Lev. xiv. 8 9; xv. 5, 6, 7, 8, 10, 11, 13, 16, 18, 21, 22, 27; xvi. 4, 24, 26, 28; xvii. 15; xxii. 6. Num. xix. 7, 8, 19.

But were these bathings or washings immersions? When we consider the scrupulous exactness of the Jews in conforming to the ritual of the law, and take in connection with this the fact that immersion of the body in water is the common eastern mode of bathing, there need be but little doubt that these bathings were real immersions.

But we have more conclusive evidence.

Maimonides, the greatest of Jewish Rabbis, who ought to know the customs of his own nation, says:—

"Whenever in the law washings occur, either of the flesh or of the garments from defilement, nothing else is to be understood than the immersion of the whole body in a bath. And that which is said 'he shall not wash his hands in water,' is to be understood as if he said he must immerse his whole body in water. And after the same order shall other impurities be judged of, so that if one should immerse himself all over except the extremity of his little finger, he is yet in his uncleanness."*

Dean Stanley:—

"The plunge into the bath of purification, long known among the Jewish nation as a symbol of a change of life, was still continued (in baptism)."†

Cremer, in his masterly Biblico Theological Lexicon of the New Testament Greek, acknowledged by scholars to be without a peer in its special sphere, says:—

"The peculiar and Christian use of the word *(baptizo)* to denote *immersion, submersion* for a religious purpose = to baptize, John i. 25, may be pretty clearly traced back to the Levitical washings. Heb. *Rachats*, Lev. xiv. 8, 9; xv. 5, 6, 7, 8, 10, 11, etc.∥ So also Dr. Alting, Com. Heb. p. 260; Lightfoot in Clark's Com. Mark; Dr. Kitto, etc."

Let us sum up. On the one hand there are at least thirty, perhaps seventy, distinct cases of washing or bathing in the Old Testament, which were to all intents and purposes immersions. These immersions were repeated among all the people times without number. We hold that the "divers baptisms" referred to these "divers immersions," the word baptize being thus used in its ordinary and universal acceptation. On the other hand,

---

* Hilch. Mikva 1, 2.   † Baptism.   ∥ Art. Baptism.

there was but one case of sprinkling in general and continual practice. Yet those who wish to make baptism a sprinkling would have us believe that the apostle applied the term "divers" to this one case, and the extraordinary one of the leper, and that he also in this verse passed by the word *rantismos*, which he ever uses elsewhere to denote the sprinklings of the law, and which meant nothing else, and uses *baptismos*, which always means immerse, and never sprinkle. The reader can judge which is the most reasonable view.

Not only so, but pure unmixed water was never used in any Old Testament sprinkling. Wherever water alone is used in the Old Testament it is a bathing—which we have found to be an immersion. If, then, John's baptism is proved to be a legal purification by John iii. 25, it is all the worse for sprinkling; for this baptism was of water only, and it must therefore have been an immersion.

Note.—Mr. McKay seems to regard purifications of the Old Testament as symbols of physical cleansing, rather than physical cleansings as symbols of inner purification. To state this idea is sufficient to refute it. He also must believe that these washings and bathings were performed by sprinkling. How he can do this when he knows that, in many instances of personal purifications, the Old Testament writers declare that there was first a sprinkling followed by a bathing, I do not know. If the last, which is designated a washing in distinction to the first sprinkling, is nevertheless a sprinkling, why did they use a different word, and why did those learned Jews who translated the original Hebrew into Greek in the Septuagint, use different words also?

In his last reply, Mr. McKay attempts to evade the force of this argument. The terming it a "literary curiosity" may pass as the harmless resort of one who can do no better. He objects to reference to the washing of clothes as pertaining to "carnal ordinances." Carnal means pertaining to the flesh. Does not the cleanness or uncleanness of the clothes have to do with the flesh? There are enough references to the washings of the body itself for the argument, if any object to the other class of passages. He states that "most of his (Prof. Goodspeed's) quotations for the washing of clothes are connected with the cleansing of the leper and other sprinklings, which he had already eliminated from the 'divers baptisms'." This statement is false in two particulars. I did not rule out the case of the leper, and none of the quotations are connected with sprinklings, I did rule out. Mr. McKay says: "In his 'washings of the whole body,' his quotations are equally unfortunate. In every one of them, with a single exception (Lev. xiv. 8), there is no preposition '*in*'—but the naked instrumental *hudati* (with water), and very few of them make any mention of being washings of *all* the flesh; most of them are connected with the leprosy in its cleansing." There are just two of the twenty-three quotations "connected with the leprosy." The reader need only turn up the passages to judge whether "*all* the flesh" was to be washed. Need I add, that I referred to the original Hebrew and not to the Septuagint translation? Remembering that many of these washings succeeded a sprinkling, even if we allow that they mean washing or bathing with water rather than in water, it will not help Mr. McKay much in his attempt to prove that these washings which are thus distinguished from the sprinklings as another part of the ceremony and by another word, were really sprinklings, and there were two sprinklings and no bathing, thus making our Bible, and much more, the Hebrew text, state an untruth.

In his own characteristic way, he says, "these washings were not 'physical scrubbings,' but 'symbolic cleansings'"; but they are called washings, all the same, and sometimes in contradistinction to sprinklings. What might have been does not so much concern us, as what is. All we need to know, in this connection, is, that these washings were not sprinklings, as Mr McKay would have his readers believe. So much for the reply.

Our author makes the usual point about the

BAPTISM IN THE CLOUD AND IN THE SEA,

and waxes merry over the idea of being immersed on dry ground. If there were no element but *water* in which immersion could occur, his remarks would be in place. The Israelites were surrounded by the sea and cloud so as to be completely enveloped in them, just as in baptism one is enveloped by water. So evidently does this reference to baptism favor immersion as its mode, that Dr. Schaff, the most learned Presbyterian of America, the editor of Lange's Commentary, and one of the American board of revision, in the quotation elsewhere given, inserts "the comparison of baptism with the passage through the Red Sea" among the proofs that Scripture baptism was an immersion. Lange says, "The cloud is, in a measure, taken together with the water as the element into which they entered, and wherein they became as it were submerged."†

Alford says, commenting on the clause "Received baptism unto Moses," "Entered by the act of such immersion," etc., and "They passed under both (cloud and sea) as the baptized passes under water."‡

Meyer, commenting on the clause "In the cloud and in the sea," says, "In" is local, as in Matt. iii. 11, denoting the element in which the performance of the baptism took place through immersion and emersion (Ein-und Hervortauchen).§

Fausset, "There is a resemblance between the symbols also: for the cloud and sea consist of water, and as these took the Israelites out of sight and then restored them again to view, so the water does to the baptized."‖ Had we space we could quote Pool, Bengel, Whitley, Olshausen, Bloomfield, Moses Stuart, and other Pedobaptist scholars to the same effect. The interpretation which is thus adopted by the foremost exegetes of the past and present cannot be made to appear absurd by

---

† Com. in Loco.   ‡ Com. in Loco.   § Com. in Loco.
‖ Com. in Loco.

Mr. McKay. There is more danger, under such circumstances, that Mr. McKay be made to appear absurd.

Need we refer to the attempt to make this passage refer to sprinkling by associating with it the expression, "the clouds poured out water," Ps. lxxvii. 17. Serious argument in this case is out of the question. The baptism was "*in the cloud and in the sea,*" not by rain from a cloud, according to Paul.

THE BAPTISM OF THE THREE THOUSAND AT PENTECOST.

This is supposed to be a case where immersion was impossible. Let us notice the objections, which have been answered so often.

1. *Want of time to immerse so many.* Probably this would have been omitted, had not Mr. McKay made a mistake in his figures. He says, "But to have immersed them all in five hours, each of the one hundred and twenty disciples there assembled must have immersed more than fifty persons every hour."* They would have required to immerse just *five* every hour, not fifty. It would be no great task surely to do this.

2. *Want of water in Jerusalem.*

Yet Dr. Robinson, who urges the objection, states† that Jerusalem was watered by the following pools with these large dimensions:—

	LENGTH.	BREADTH.	DEPTH.
Bethesda	360	130	75 feet.
Siloam	53	18	19 "
Upper Pool	316	218	18 "
Hezekiah	240	144	partly filled.
Lower Pool	592	260	40 feet.

* In his last edition, Mr. McKay, determined to make a point, in some way, quietly assumes that only the twelve could baptize, and, of course, he thinks it impossible for them to have immersed so many in the time. As our Lord had commissioned the one hundred and twenty to baptize, and they were here present, he should tell us why they might not have assisted the apostles.

† See Robinson's Lexicon of N. Test. Greek, Art. *baptizo.*

"But in addition to these," continues Dr. R., "almost every private house in Jerusalem of any size, is understood to have at least one or more cisterns. The house of Mr. Lanneau, in which we resided, had no less than four cisterns, and as these are but a specimen of the manner in which all the better class of houses is supplied, I subjoin here the dimensions":*—

	LENGTH.	BREADTH.	DEPTH.
I.	15	8	12 feet.
II.	8	4	15 "
III.	10	10	15 "
IV.	30	30	20* "

There was no lack of water then.

3. *These reservoirs and pools were not available for baptism.*

Dean Stanley and Dr. Hackett, both men of wide learning, and both travellers in the East, think differently. Dean Stanley says, "In the early age the scene of the transaction (baptism) was either, etc., or some vast reservoir, as at Jericho or Jerusalem, whither, as in the Baths of Caracalla at Rome, the whole population resorted for swimming or washing."† Dr. Hackett declares "The habits of the East, as every traveller knows, would present no obstacle to such a use (baptism) of the public reservoirs."‡ Smith's Bib. Dic. also testifies to the same effect.§ Besides, we know from the New Testament, that Bethesda and Siloam were so used, John ix. 7 and v. 2. Neither were the people so hostile at this time as to prevent; for, Acts ii. 47, the followers of Jesus were "in favor with all the people."‖

---

* Robinson's Bib. Res. I. pp. 480-515. † Art. on Baptism. ‡ Com. in Loco. § Art. Bath.

Mr. McKay's reference to the wet clothes of the three thousand, were they immersed, pp. 33, 34, and to their robing and unrobing, etc., is not worthy of serious notice. His quotation from Dr. Dale and his own attempt at pleasantry (p. 119) over the statement, in Judea, "persons in ordinary health might plunge into the water and sit down in their wet clothes with safety and often with great comfort," might

So much for the objections that the baptism of the three thousand at Pentecost was irreconcilable with immersion.

BAPTISM BEFORE MEALS AND ON COMING FROM MARKET, LUKE XI. 38; MARK VII. 4.

Mr. McKay's criticism on the washings (baptisms) mentioned in these passages is a curiosity. He assumes roundly that the baptism of *himself* which the Pharisees expected of our Lord, Luke xi. 37, 38, was a washing of the *hands* and face. He follows this by a second assumption. Because he finds two cases, hundreds of years before, where water was poured upon the hands to wash them, he avers that this was the invariable practice. So he concludes our Lord must have baptized *himself*, by having a *servant* pour water on his *hands*, and "the exclusive immersion theory is proved to be nothing better than the baseless fabric of Baptist, etc., visions." Crushing!!

Mark vii. 3, 4, calls for further attention. The passage reads: "For the Pharisees and all the Jews, except they wash their hands oft (diligently, R. V.), eat not, holding the tradition of the elders; and when they come from market, except they wash (baptize), they eat not."

Mr. McKay, and some others, would have us believe that the washing (baptism) of v. 4, was a washing of the hands as in v. 3. They do not tell us, however, if Mark meant this, why he did not say so, instead of using another word altogether. They would also make Mark guilty of folly. As he had said in v. 3, that the Pharisees *never* ate unless they washed their hands, why did he need tell his readers in v. 4, that *when they came from*

---

well call forth a smile from the scholarly reader. He has, however, refrained from letting it be known that the above statement is given in my pamphlet as a quotation from the learned Dr. P. Smith. There are few who would care to attempt to ridicule anything from this scholar's pen, lest they make themselves ridiculous.

market they did not eat unless they washed their hands? The Evangelist evidently, in v. 4, refers to a case where something more is done than usual, because the supposed defilement is greater. In ordinary cases, it suffices to wash the hands, but on contact with the unclean in the market, they must baptize. Meyer puts it well: "'Except they wash' (baptize), is not to be understood of the *washing of the hands*, but of *immersion* (Eintauchen), which the word in the classics and in the New Testament everywhere means, here, according to the context, *to take a bath*. . . The statement is in the form of a climax Before eating they *always* wash the hands. If they would eat *on coming from market*, however, *they take a bath*."*

BAPTISM OF VESSELS AND TABLES, MARK VII. 4.

Pedobaptist friends who have been told repeatedly that this passage is utterly inconsistent with immersion will be surprised to learn that there are no grounds for this assertion.

On this passage we remark:—

1. Mr. McKay does not give us his authority for the assertion that these tables (couches) were usually twenty feet long, four high and four broad. Smith's Bib. Dic., the best authority, declares that these couches were often of matting, etc., without frames, and that the frames, when used, were "*slight and portable*."

2. "Couches" is left out, as without sufficient MS. authority, in the Revised Version.

3. Maimonides, the great Jewish Rabbi, who knew the customs of his own people perfectly, says:—

"Every vessel of wood which is made for the use of man, as a table, etc., receives defilement."

And he adds, further on,—

---

* Com. in Loco.

"A bed that is wholly defiled, if he dip it part by part, it is pure."—Hilch. Celim.

Dr. Halley, a Congregationalist, in his great work on the Sacraments, says:—

"If any one will take the trouble to study the various pollutions of beds and couches, as they are described by Maimonides and the Talmudic tracts, he must in candor admit that these articles of furniture were, in some instances, immersed in water."*

So we find that it is doubtful whether Mark said that couches were baptized. If he did, the Jewish writers declare that it was customary to immerse their couches, to purify them. So this passage takes its rank among those which favor immersion, instead of bearing against it.†

THE BAPTISM OF THE SPIRIT.

We have already considered the argument which some Pedobaptists suppose is to be found in this for affusion. As it is becoming the chief dependence of

---

* In my review, through a typographical error, Dr. Halley is made to say, I *cannot deny* that the Pharisees, as early as the time of our Saviour, practised immersion after contact with the common people," instead of "*I care not to deny*," etc. Taking as much advantage as he can of this slight error, for which the printer is responsible, as I was in Europe when my pamphlet was printed and had no opportunity to correct the proof, Mr. McKay seeks to make the reader believe that my quotations and references to authorities generally are all *pretences*. The above quotation, which he does not give, will show whether Dr. Halley does not admit that furniture was immersed by the Jews, and how fair is Mr. McKay's attempt to make his readers believe that Dr. H. did not, p. 109. Mr. McKay chooses to retain this old slanderous charge in his later editions. It will help to discredit his opponent with the most of his readers, who will not read any reply.

† Mr. McKay's critical note on v. 4 is unique. He states that "the Sinaitic and Vatican manuscripts, and seven others, read *rantisontai* (sprinkle), instead of *baptisontai*, in the beginning of this verse ; thus clearly showing that the copyists deemed sprinkling and baptizing as synonymous." Now Alford and Tregelles give only the Vatican and one obscure MS. as having *rantisontai*. Let us also apply Mr. McKay's newest canon, that where N. Test. MSS. have different readings, these readings must be synonymous to a case. In James ii. 18, some MSS. have "*by* thy works," others, "*without* thy works." Justification by works and without works, therefore, mean the same thing!!

those who hold to sprinkling and pouring, and as it is fitted to impose on the thoughtless, it requires further consideration. Mr. McKay states it very well in the following sentence :—

"The baptism with the Holy Ghost is always effected by the Spirit *coming upon* the person baptized. Consequently, as water baptism is an outward sign of this inward spiritual baptism, that mode is most Scriptural and appropriate in which the element *comes upon* the person baptized."

1. It is assumed in this statement, that the water baptism is to show forth visibly the inward grace conferred by the baptism of the Spirit. What are the facts? The only baptism of the Spirit spoken of clearly in the N. Test. is that promised, Matt. iii. 11, Mark i. 8, Luke iii. 16, and effected at Pentecost, Acts i. 5 and ii. 2-5. Now mark this promise of the baptism of the Spirit our Lord himself, according to Acts i. 5, declared was for the apostles, and, perhaps, the other followers of Christ. It was realized in their being filled with the Holy Ghost, and being enabled to speak with other tongues. These had all received, already, the water baptism and the grace it signified. The water baptism coming before that of the Spirit and showing forth grace already received, could not have any reference to the grace conferred afterward, when they received the baptism of the Spirit. The baptism of the Spirit, so far as it is explained in the N. Test., was something superadded to the work on the heart, which water baptism was to show forth. This fact, which is undeniable, pierces the heart of this argument.

2. It is assumed that there was a literal affusion of the Spirit. If the expressions, the Spirit was poured out, etc., be figurative, referring to the copiousness of the influence, and it is said to descend only because of the representation of the divine abode being above us in heaven, then, as there can be no mode in the manner of the Spirit's reaching men, there can be nothing in it to

determine the mode of baptism. Can there be any doubt? Can any one, on sober thought, believe there was a literal pouring out of the Spirit? The idea is shocking. Besides, is not the Spirit omnipresent and in no need of motion to exert his energy on the soul? Finally, if there were no other representations of the manner of the Spirit's work, this material conception might be more plausible. But there are. It is said to be a well of water, John iv. 14. It is also compared to dew, and a running river. Is the Spirit literally sprinkled as well as poured? Is he drunk in as water? Is he breathed out as air? John xx. 22. Can he be literally applied in all these ways? But enough.

3. But allowing this gross material conception in the realm of the purely spiritual, and our opponents are not helped; for the "pouring out," etc., are not called the baptism. Even Dr. Robinson, in his Lexicon, in the very article on *baptizo* in which he makes a special plea for sprinkling, declares that, Matt. iii. 11, should be "baptized in the Holy Ghost," and not "baptized with the Holy Ghost," as in our Version. In the Revised Version, the American Committee, composed mostly of Pedobaptists, recommend "*in* the Holy Ghost," and it is accepted, as an alternative reading, by the English Committee. Now "baptized in the Holy Ghost" leaves no place for sprinkling or pouring as baptism, and shuts us in to immersion. The baptism is not in the mode in which the Spirit is represented as coming, for this is various; but the idea is that the disciples were permeated by the Spirit's influence and power as though they were imbathed or immersed in them. If we turn to the record of the fulfilment of this promise, Acts ii. 1-4, we find it in perfect agreement, even literally, with the meaning of the word *baptizo*, to immerse, and the terms of the promise rightly rendered. The sound which was the evidence and token of the Spirit's presence, "filled all the house where they were sitting," and "they were filled with the Holy Ghost." Cyril, one of the Church Fathers,

writing about A.D. 350, puts it well in his highly wrought way: "The house became the reservoir of the spiritual water: the disciples were sitting within: and the whole house was filled. They were therefore completely immersed according to the promise." We could quote Theophylact, Neander, Moses Stuart, Lange, and others to the same effect, but we forbear.

4. Again, still allowing the idea that there was a literal "pouring out" of the Spirit, it must further be established that water baptism is to symbolize the mode of the Spirit's coming upon the soul, before the fact of the Spirit's coming in a certain form will stamp that form on water baptism. But even on this supposition, what imaginable purpose could be served by an ordinance to keep men reminded that the Spirit, in its operation upon the soul, comes down upon it, and does not come in another way? To suppose baptism for such a purpose would be to impute folly to the All-Wise. Besides, if the outward sign was to conform to the mode in which the Spirit's work is said to be done, rather than to symbolize the *effects* of that work on the nature, Heb. x. 22 would be "Having our hearts sprinkled from an evil conscience, and our bodies *sprinkled* with pure water." But as Heb. x. 22 reads, "Having our hearts sprinkled from an evil conscience, and our bodies *washed* with pure water," God's word decides against this idea.

5. But if we rule out the idea that there was a literal pouring out of the Spirit, then the pouring out is a figurative representation of the Spirit's plenteous influences, and Mr. McKay's contention would make baptism the symbol of the figurative description of the Spirit's operation—or of one of its descriptions. What a wonderful purpose this would make the form of baptism serve!! God gave it a certain form that it might symbolize the figurative representation of the Spirit's manner of operation! Who dare impute such folly to our Heavenly Father?

6. The true symbolism of baptism destroys this argument for sprinkling or pouring, root and branch. Baptism is, as Mr. McKay, agreeing with his own Westminster Confession, Chap. XXVIII, 1, asserts, to symbolize the Spirit's work of regeneration in the soul He makes a statement as wide of the mark as it could well be, however, when he declares that Baptists do not believe this. They are the only people who hold this view consistently, since all but them apply baptism to infants in whom there is no such work to be symbolized by baptism, unless it first regenerates. Well, then, if baptism symbolizes the work of the Spirit in the soul, how can he make it show forth the mode of the Spirit's coming upon the soul ? What this symbol of regeneration is we know from Rom. vi. 3-5, where baptism is said to be a burial to symbolize the death to sin and resurrection to newness of life which regeneration effects. We know also that it is a complete washing, Titus iii. 5, to symbolize that purification which makes one a new creature in Christ Jesus.

7. But the idea that the descent of the Spirit is the baptism, makes nonsense, when applied to the passages involved. John i. 32, would read, "I saw the Spirit baptizing from heaven like a dove." Acts ii. 17, "I will baptize of my Spirit upon all flesh." Acts ii. 33, "He has baptized this which ye now see," etc, which would make it appear that the element is the object baptized, and prevent the baptism of the people altogether.

8. This boasted argument for sprinkling and pouring then, is found to be based upon the revolting assumption that the Spirit is poured out literally, and that water baptism is to show forth the mode of the Spirit's descent, thus setting aside its deep and blessed import—thus denying that it is to symbolize a work of grace in the soul, and reducing references to it to an absurdity. For the sake of such an argument we are asked to set aside an interpretation which is consistent in all its parts, and

which harmonizes with the meaning which baptize ever had, and accept for baptism a signification the word never bore. Can our Pedobaptist friends wonder that we cannot yield to the force of such an argument as this, but are surprised that they should esteem it of any strength.

CHAPTER IV.—THE ARGUMENT FROM SCRIPTURE.

PROOF FOR IMMERSION.

The word *baptizo* is used once in a literal way in the Septuagint. As the Septuagint is the Old Testament translated into Hellenistic Greek, the Greek in which the New Testament is written, this case possessed a peculiar interest. It is

NAAMAN'S SEVENFOLD BAPTISM, II KINGS V. 14.

The Seventy here use *baptizo* to translate the Hebrew word *taval*. If the word *taval*, then, means to immerse, these learned Jews must have regarded immerse as the meaning of baptize. The word *taval* is used fifteen times in the Old Testament, viz.: Gen. xxxvii. 31, Exod. xii. 22, Lev. iv. 6, ix. 9, xiv. 6, 51, Deut. xxxiii. 24, Num. xix. 18, Josh. iii. 15, I Sam. ix. 27, II Kings v. 14, viii. 15, Job ix. 31, Ezek. xxiii. 15. In all these cases, except the two last, the learned men who translated our Bible render it to dip. And in these cases it is the equivalent of dip: for in Job ix. 31, it is plunge, and in Ezek. xxiii. 15, it is dyed, viz., by dipping. Gesenius in his Hebrew Lexicon defines it, to dip, to dip in, to immerse. So do Maurer, Gibbs, Ainsworth, and Simon in their Lexicons, and McClintock and Strong in their Encyclopædia. So also do Stokins and Leigh, and Schindler, who substantially agree in Stokins' definition, "properly it is to immerse (intingere) anything so that it touches the liquid in whole or merely in part. So it is said of the priests dipping the finger or other things in blood, Lev. iv. 6, 17, ix. 9," etc.*

But yet Mr. McKay tries to prove that in the case of Naaman it was a sprinkling. How strange, if this were so, that the Hebrew word for sprinkle was not used, and that one was substituted which never meant to sprinkle, but always to dip! But how does he seek to make this appear? He says the prophet "would command him to do what the law of God prescribes: this was sprinkling seven times." Now mark! The law, Lev. xiv., prescribed what lepers who were already cured should do to declare that they were healed. But Naaman's was no instance of such a case, for he was still diseased, and Elisha enjoined what was miraculously to cure him, II Kings v. 10, 11. The law made no provision for such a case. But after having assumed that the Levitical observances would be enjoined upon Naaman by Elisha, and upon my reminding him in my review that, in Lev. xiv., the sprinkling was but a small part of the ceremony, which was consummated in a bathing, he assumes further, that the rest of the ceremonies were omitted because he was not a Jew. What convenient logic! Elisha is first made, in order to get in sprinkling, to enjoin for the cure of a leper what the law prescribed in an altogether different case. Then, to keep out the bathing or washing, which would be most inconvenient, he assumes that Elisha did not enjoin all that the law prescribed, even in that case. Finally, while the command was to wash *(rachats)*, and a part of the Mosaic ritual was a washing, Lev. xiv. 8, prescribed by the same word *(rachats)*, Mr. McKay declares that this very washing is what Naaman was

---

* Mr. Ditzler, in the Graves-Ditzler Debate, p. 87, assumes, because these Lexicographers say that *taval* refers thus to partial immersion, it does not mean immerse, Lev. iv. 6, 17, ix. 9. But the part is always immersed, to which *taval* refers. This is enough. He also translates the Latin *tinxit*, in the definitions of Lexicographers who wrote in that language, by moisten, which is not the sense in which they used it. *Tingo, intingo* with them mean dip, dip in.

allowed to omit when he was commanded to wash, and that Elisha intended him to sprinkle himself and not wash, when he told him to wash. Why then did he not tell him to sprinkle, using the Hebrew word which ever meant sprinkle, and not one which is distinguished from sprinkle in numberless cases, and never conveyed this idea? Is it possible for patience and charity to meet the demands which such apparent attempts to wrest the Scriptures from their plain meaning, make upon us? How simple it is if we take the incident as it reads. Naaman was commanded to wash seven times in Jordan. He obeyed this command by dipping himself in the Jordan seven times. This Hebrew word for "dip" is translated by the Seventy baptize, thus proving that they thought baptism a dipping.*

NOTE.—Mr. Lathern, Baptisma, p. 145, following the example of some others, refers to two cases of the use of *baptizo* in the Apocrypha. The first is that of Judith, Judith xii. 5, sq., where this Jewish maiden received permission from Holofernes to pass the body guards with her maid, and repair by night to a fountain in the camp and bathe (baptize) herself, and pray. Dr. Wilson, whom Mr. L. quotes with approval, supposes this fountain the source of the water supply of the army, and that it would not be seemly for a maiden to immerse herself there. But would it have been seemly, under such circumstances, for her to have bathed in any way, at such a place? The fact that she went by night—that she went to pray as well as to bathe—that did she but wish to bathe in any other way than immersion, she might have done so from a basin in her tent—show both that the fountain must have been secluded, and that she immersed herself, as the word used to describe the transaction signifies.

---

* Mr. McKay waxes quite indignant over our version of the Bible because it contains such "blundering translations" as "dipped himself," "bathe in water," "went down into the water," "came up out of the water," "much water," etc. The Revised Version, the work of those who were supposed to be the ablest scholars in England and America, has retained every one of these "blundering translations," and yet, Mr. McKay, with that confidence in his own superior knowledge which gives him such self-complacency even when making statements which would cause those the world recognizes as its greatest scholars to blush, retains this charge against these learned men.

BAPTISM: AN ARGUMENT AND A REPLY. 51

The other case is mentioned in Wisdom of Sirach xxxiv. 27, "Baptizing himself from a dead body, and touching it again, what is he profited by his bathing?" which Mr. L. explains, "The sprinkling of the unclean, which according to inspired teaching, sanctified, was understood in the 'Wisdom of Sirach' to be a baptism."

Not so fast. Let us turn to Num. xix. 19, where the ceremony referred to is mentioned, and to which the reader is not referred. It is there said that the **defiled** person shall first be sprinkled upon, and then *bathe himself.* Are we to believe that the expression, "what is he profited by his bathing," does not refer to the bathing of Num. xix. 19, but to the sprinkling? When the readers are referred to the facts, I am sure they cannot accept such a statement.

I am sorry to find that Dr. Hodge, vol. iii. 529, has committed the same oversight. He refers the reader to as much of the description in Num. xix. as relates to the sprinkling, and then assumes that this was the baptism from the dead body. Had he given the rest of the verse in Sirach, "what is he profited by his bathing," and referred the reader to Num. xix. 19, where washing is enjoined after the sprinkling, the reader would have seen that the baptism was a bathing—an immersion, as Maimonides and the Talmudists testify.

THE BAPTISM OF JOHN.

The facts about John's baptism are these, Matt. iii. 6, Mark i. 5. "They were baptized in the river Jordan." Mark i. 9 (Jesus) "was baptised of John *into* the Jordan," *eis ton Jordanen,* (see Revised Version, margin). John iii. 23, "And John was baptizing in Ænon near to Salem because there was much water there." In all these passages the New Version translation is given. So the reader can see what the result of the latest and best scholarship on the question of the prepositions is. The fact that John resorted to the Jordan, and to Ænon, because of its plentiful waters, in order to baptize, most clearly indicates that baptism was an immersion, which requires a larger quantity of water, and not sprinkling, which requires but a few quarts for thousands. The fact also that they were not only baptized in the Jordan but *into* the Jordan, proves conclusively that John's baptism was an immersion, and not a sprinkling. Here at least, *eis* can have no meaning but "into," even with those who think baptism a sprinkling or pouring. Sprinkled or poured " to," " up to," or " unto," the Jordan cannot hold. But taking the only meaning of which *eis* is here capable, viz.: " into," sprinkling and pouring are out of the question. Sprinkled or poured *into* the Jordan makes nonsense. Nothing but immersed into the Jordan can here make sense. *Baptized into the Jordan (eis ton Jordanen)* can mean nothing else than that John did put our Lord into the water of the Jordan. When we consider that the word baptize, in every case of its literal use meant to immerse, and that it never meant sprinkle, the fact that all the prepositions and circumstances are in exact harmony with this act, while they are all out of harmony with sprinkle, is enough to settle the question in the minds of all who know the facts, and are open to conviction.

But upon what does Mr. McKay and others depend to break the force of this argument? How do they seek to make it appear that baptize was used to describe an act which in all its previous use, it had never done?

1. He assumes that John's baptizing was the exercise of his office as priest in sprinkling the people according to the promise in Ezekiel xxxvi. 25. " I will sprinkle clean water upon you." But John himself, Jn. i. 33, declares that he baptized not because he belonged to the priestly class, but by virtue of a special commission from God. Where is there any hint in scripture that priests sprinkled unmixed water in any of their rites? Sprinkling was always of blood or water mixed with ashes. Where is the faintest intimation that priests exercised any office of sprinkling at the Jordan or in secluded places? Where is there the remotest hint that they did this for the purposes of John's baptism? Where is

there any evidence that the people regarded his baptism as the recognized work of a priest? How could John fulfil the promise, "I will sprinkle clean water upon you," whatever the prophecy means, when we remember that the "I" who was to sprinkle was God and not John?

2. He assumes that the baptism of John was in conformity with the Levitical purifications with water, which he avers were invariably sprinklings. We have already seen that the exact opposite of this is the truth, there being no sprinkling of unmixed water in the Levitical rites. Wherever water is used it is as a bathing, which Maimonides and the Talmudists, the best authorities, declare was an immersion. But if John sprinkled, why then did the evangelists not use *antizo*, as the Septuagint and the Epistle to the Hebrews always do to signify sprinkle, and not *baptizo*, which is never used in that sense?

3. He declares, since baptized in the wilderness, etc., does not mean under the wilderness, therefore, baptized in Jordan does not mean under its waters. What surprising acuteness!

4. But he avers "in the river Jordan" does not mean in the river at all, because, in the Old Testament, there are instances where Jordan is used of the district beside the Jordan. But in neither of these cases is the term "river Jordan" used. This makes all the difference. If we said, some one was baptized in St. Lawrence it might mean a place, but if we said, in the river St. Lawrence there could be no doubt. So here.

But the attempt to make it appear that river Jordan does not mean the river has overlooked one fact. Mark i. 9, says "Baptized into *(eis)* the Jordan." Now no sleight-of-hand with the preposition *eis*, can make sense, if "Jordan" be not the river but a place. Allow that it means "to," or "up to," or "unto," and the clause reads, "and was baptized of John to, up to, unto, the land of

Jordan," which is nonsense. Nothing but baptized *into* the Jordan will make sense. But if the preposition "into" must be used, so must the baptism, when we are shut in to sprinkle, pour, or immerse, be immersion. Pour, or sprinkle into the Jordan will not do. Immerse into makes complete sense. On p. 45 Mr. McKay says, "In 1 King i. 33, 38, 45, we read that Solomon was anointed *eis* Gihon, (a river, 2 Chron. xxxii. 30; xxxiii. 14); and in Mark i. 9, we read that Jesus was baptized *eis ton Jordanen* (a river). No one will say that the *anointing* was by '*immersion,*' 1 King i. 39. Why then contend that the baptism must have been by immersion, when it is precisely the same form of expression that is used." Mr. McKay has been misled. There is no expression "anointed *eis* Gihon," as there is baptizing *eis* the Jordan. Solomon is *brought down eis* Gihon (a place, Smith's Bib. Dic.) and anointed there. That is all.

5. Mr. McKay, following the example of a certain type of controversialists, seeks to reduce the "much water" at Ænon, to "many springs." He says, "There is not a scholar in the world to-day, unless he is in bondage to the dipping theory, who would translate "*polla hudata*" "much water." Unfortunately for this confident assertion, the translators of the Revised Version, in no bondage to "dipping," have retained the "much water" as the translation of "*polla hudata.*" The other instances of its New Testament use are Rev. iv. 15, xiv. 2, xvii. 1, xix. 6, in each of which the substitution of "many springs" for "many waters" would make nonsense. Dr. Thompson speaking of Beisan, in the neighborhood of which Ænon was, says, "All kinds of machinery might be driven with the least possible expense by its abounding brooks," etc.[*]

6. His attempts to make it appear that the representation of the baptism of the Spirit is inconsistent

---

[*]Land and the Book, p. 456.

with immersion, have already been answered, as also his reference to it as a Mosaic purification.

7. He assumes because in the Septuagint it is sometimes said anoint *(en)* oil when the oil is poured, therefore baptized in *(en)* water may mean poured with water. But it is said baptized *(en)* the river Jordan. Here *(en)* cannot mean with. Poured with the river Jordan or sprinkled with the river Jordan will not do. *En* here has its usual meaning of "in." And if John baptized in the river Jordan, can there be a doubt that it was by immersion?

8. The physical impossibility that John should immerse so many is assumed. The most Pedobaptist writers who urge this time-worn objection, do not venture to enlarge the whole population of Judah and Jerusalem to more than two or three millions. Mr. McKay makes it five. In reply we remark, the disciples of John may have assisted him, the expression "baptized by John" being similar to "the ark was built by Noah." Luke vii. 3, Matt. xx. 25, John iv. 1, i. 11, iii. 23, prove that Matt. iii. 5, probably means no more than John xii. 32. "And I if I be lifted up will draw all men unto me," viz.: that there were many of all classes baptized by John.

9. The wet garments would present little trouble. Dr. Payne Smith says "In Jordan, during the larger part of the year, persons in ordinary health might plunge into the water and sit down in their wet clothes with safety, and often with comfort and pleasure"

Thus we have followed this pamphlet in all its rash and puerile statements—statements which demand notice only because they might be supposed unanswerable by the unlearned, if left unanswered—statements to which resort should not be made in Christian controversy. And we find that the description of the baptism of John are absolutely inconsistent with anything but immersion. There is a fallacy in all such attempts which should be borne in mind. If they can in any way, by wresting the prepositions from their usual meaning, etc., make it possible that the descriptions of baptism might have been ought else than an immersion, certain Pedobaptists assume that baptism was by sprinkling or pouring. But they know that the word baptism never meant sprinkle or pour, and always meant immerse. Such being the case, what right have they to aver that an unusual meaning of the prepositions must be assumed in order that a meaning it never had be forced on baptize? Under such circumstances we are only permitted to give the strange meaning of sprinkle or pour to baptize, if the descriptions of it absolutely make it impossible to give it its otherwise invariable meaning of immerse. How strange then, when the whole description of baptism is just what we should expect were it an immersion, to force unusual meanings on the prepositions in order to force a meaning it never had on baptize?

In his revised pamphlet, Mr. McKay has abandoned the position criticised in my reply to his first,—that our Lord's baptism was his consecration to the priesthood. In this he seeks to make capital out of the fact that in the account of our Lord's baptism, Matt. 3: 16 the preposition *apo* is used, and the Revised Version translate the clause, "And Jesus, when he was baptized, went up straightway from the water," not "out of" the water. Baptists, according to his own showing, have been the first to admit the correct rendering of *apo* in this clause to be "from" and not "out of." Mr. McKay should have stated, however, that in the account of the baptism in Mark 1; 10 the preposition used is *ek*, and that the Revised Version translates this, "And straightway coming up *out of* the water," etc. Now going up "from" the water does not deny that our Lord may have been in the water, while coming up "out of" the water does deny that he went merely to the water's edge. The only explanation, therefore, which harmonizes the two accounts of our Lord's baptism is the one which leaves no reasonable ground for sprinkling and pouring, but permits us to give to *baptizo* its invariable meaning of immerse.

Mr. McKay also asserts that our Lord was baptized with the Holy Ghost, and that the mode is declared by the passages: "The Spirit of God *descended* like a dove, and lighted upon him." "God annointed Jesus of Nazareth with the Holy Ghost." Our Lord was baptized before the Holy Ghost lighted upon him as a dove. Baptism then was not a symbol of what was already done, but a type of what was to be! Surely this is a new idea of baptism?

THE BAPTISM OF THE EUNUCH, ACTS 8: 38, 39.

The account reads in the Revised Version "And they both went down into the water, both Philip and the eunuch, and he baptized him. And when they came up out of the water," etc. Can a description be plainer of what happens in an immersion? Can the description hold of sprinkling or pouring? Do candidates and administrator go down into, and come up out of the water in the case of sprinkling? Is there any reason why they should?

But Mr. McKay, as usual, takes issue with these learned scholars who have given us our revised version. He declares it should have read, "went down *to* the water, and came up *from* the water." Which will the reader hold as the greater authority, Mr. McKay or the learned revisers? A word about the prepositions in this verse. While *eis* "into" may possibly mean "unto," in a very few very exceptional cases, the preposition *ek*, "out of," never means "from the side of." This can be seen by the unlearned reader from the fact that there is a separate Greek preposition *apo* to express motion from beside, as distinguished from *ek* "out of the midst of." So Dr. Robinson in his Greek Lexicon of the New Testament, says of *ek* " Primary signification *out of, from, of,* Lat. *e, ex,* spoken of such objects as before were *in* or *within* another, but are now separated from it." Of *apo* he says "It marks in strictness the separation of such objects only as were before *on, at, by, near, with* another, externally ; not *in* or *within* another, for in respect of such *ek* is used."

And yet, this writer has the hardihood to assert that *ek* is here used to mean " from beside," which it never meant, while there was *apo* at hand which never had any other meaning.

But after having by *such* ways, made it appear that Philip and the eunuch did not enter the water, he proceeds to prove that the baptism was a sprinkling on dry ground, thus

" Immersionists, instead of ignorantly dwelling upon unusual !! and false !!! translations," (what dunces the translators of the new version must be), " to prove their theory, would do well to follow a better way. If they will examine their Bibles they will see that the eunuch was on this occasion reading a passage of Isaiah (there was no division into chapters and verses then) in which it is predicted of Christ, among other things, that 'He shall sprinkle many nations,' etc. As Philip was explaining this Scripture to him they came to a certain water ; and the eunuch said 'See! water (the words indicate that the quantity was small, and that Philip was likely to pass it by unnoticed) what doth hinder me to be baptized (*i.e.* sprinkled), since this great Saviour has come who was to sprinkle many nations, and I am one of those He was to sprinkle.'"

Baptists do examine their Bibles, all the worse for such a statement.* Acts viii. 32 says that the eunuch was reading " He was led as a lamb to the slaughter,

---

*Mr. McKay has omitted this statement from his later editions. It is retained here because many of his pamphlets containing it are still in circulation. In his last revision, he declares that where it is stated, they both " went down," it means from the chariot. We do

etc.," Isaiah liii. 7, not "He shall sprinkle many nations" which is in Isaiah lii. 15. Even though he had been reading this, and allowing this to be the correct translation, how would the work of Christ on the hearts of men which this expression refers to, suggest an outward rite of sprinkling. The outward rite which corresponds can be seen in Heb. x. 22, "Having our hearts sprinkled from an evil conscience, and *our bodies washed with pure water.*" *

THE PREPOSITIONS IN GENERAL.

The ordinary reader can be easily confused about the meaning of these. Mr. McKay and a certain class of controversialists, adopt this method. They gather together two or three, or perhaps half a dozen instances of a most unusual meaning of a preposition. They, however, do not say that this is a most extraordinary use of the word. Thus their readers are left to infer that this is the ordinary, and not the extraordinary signification, and conclude that the prepositions are against us.

Let me give the reader a few facts about the prepositions involved in this question.

The Greek preposition *eis*, both in the old and new version is invariably translated "into," when it has to

---

not care to admit Mr. McKay's right to add to the word of God. In this case, however, he would need to take away as well as add. "Went down" corresponds with "came up." If they both merely "went down" from the chariot, they both, when they went up, went up into the chariot. But we are told that Philip was caught away, and did not go up into the chariot, therefore, the expression went down, does not refer to descending from it.

* Mr. Lathern, Baptisma, p. 53, declares that the way over which the eunuch was passing to Gaza was through a desert where "no man has ever found foaming flood or water deep enough for submersion." Mr. Thompson who spent about a score of years in Palestine as a Congregationalist missionary tells us, "Land and the Book" p, 536, "He (Philip) would have met the chariot somewhere South East of Latron. There is a fine stream of water called Marubbah, deep enough even in June to satisfy the utmost wishes of our Baptist friends."

do with baptism. Therefore, according to the judgment of these translators who represent the best scholarship of the seventeenth and nineteenth centuries, this preposition has the meaning which favors or proves immersion, and which is irreconcilable with any other mode.

In the Gospels and Acts, where the administration of baptism alone is mentioned, and which we need alone examine on the point, *eis* is translated "in" or "into" five hundred and thirty-six times. In addition to this, there are one hundred and seventy cases where it is translated "to" or "unto" where people are spoken of as going "to" or "unto" a place or house, and meaning of course "into," for the people or person entered the house or town in every case, thus swelling the number to about seven hundred. And how often does the reader suppose *eis* is used in the sense of "to" or "unto" when there can be any doubt? Not more than a score of times. In its use in reference to water, the case involved in this question, there is but *one* instance of this kind—that mentioned by Mr. McKay, Matt. xvii. 27, "Go thou *eis* the sea." But even in this case, it may mean that Peter was to go out into the sea, as we sometimes say, even in English, in his boat. What strange procedure, then, to give these instances of the use of *eis* which occur only once in fifty or one hundred cases, leave it to be inferred that this is the ordinary use and then assume an air of triumph, as though the Baptist position had been overthrown. How strange, especially when we know that this is an attempt to force a meaning upon baptize which it never had: force an almost unexampled meaning upon *eis* in order that it may agree with a still more unexampled signification of baptize, while the almost invariable meaning of both would leave them in perfect harmony. Need we say more.

The preposition *en*. The meaning of this preposition which favors immersion, and is inconsistent with sprinkling or pouring, is "in." The meaning which will permit affusion, but which does not exclude immersion, is "with." In the Gospels and Acts it is translated "in" nine hundred and twenty times, and "with" only twenty-nine times. Of these twenty-nine times, it refers to baptism nine times. In these nine cases, the American revisors, supposed to be the finest scholars on this continent, advised that it should be translated "in" water, Holy Ghost, and fire, in every instance, and the English revisors accept this as an alternative reading. The other twenty passages where "with" is found, are all cases of figurative usage, and have no bearing on the question at issue. So again we find that, in the attempts to make *en* inconsistent with immersion, and favorable to sprinkling, a meaning is assumed to be its general one, which is almost unexampled in the relation in question, and this most unusual meaning thus forced upon *en* is used to reconcile it with a signification which baptize never bore, although the almost invariable meaning of both *en* and *baptizo* are in perfect accord as related in the passages in question.*

We have already discussed *ek*. We may add that it is most usually translated from, when spoken of motion away from a place, but in every such case the person or thing goes from within, and not from beside. This latter idea is exactly expressed by *apo*. Even in its tropical use, the idea of "out of" is invariably seen. This is true of the cases which Mr. McKay has chosen as most inconsistent with this meaning, viz., Rom. i. 17, Matt. xii. 23, John x. 22.

Thus the testimony of the prepositions is clear and unwavering. Instead of the translations of them in the old version being too favorable to immersion, and blunders, the new is still more favorable, and all the childish criticism goes for naught.

---

*Mr. Lathern, Baptisma, p. 24-30, discusses the use of the preposition *en* and states as the first of his conclusions "That the preposition *en*, governing the dative of locality, denoting 'rest in a place,' means what we express by the word *at*." This is to make baptized *in* the Jordan *at* the Jordan. The criticism he makes upon the first

Chapter V.—The Argument from Scripture Concluded.

Buried by Baptism, Rom. VI. 3, 5; Col. II. 12.

1. Almost all commentators and critics of all ages, and of every name, regard these passages as conclusive for immersion as baptism. The few who think they refer to the work of the Spirit on the heart, believe, for the most part, that this inner work is described in language drawn from the outward act, and, therefore, that the proof for immersion in the fact that baptism is called a burial, is the same. It is difficult to see how this can be doubted. Why should this spiritual and invisible work on the heart be called a burial by baptism? There can be no actual burial in what is spiritual. It could be for no other reason than that the water baptism is a burial, and that, therefore, the spiritual change is, in a figurative way, described through the act which represents it. If baptism were a sprinkling, Paul says here "Buried by sprinkling" which cannot be reconciled with common sense, whether spoken of what is material or spiritual, outward or inward. Well may Bp. Hoadley say:

"If baptism had been then performed as it is now among us. (by sprinkling) we should never so much as heard of such a form of expression, of dying and rising again in this rite."*

Mr. McKay, therefore, in supposing that he has destroyed the force of these passages for immersion, by

---

example cited to sustain this statement, will be enough to show its character, "*en to eremo*," "*at* the *desert*" encampment, not *under* the desert sand. "At the desert" as preferable to "in the desert," because "in the desert" must mean *under* it." I shall not add one word.

*Works III. p. 890.

making them refer to so called spiritual baptism, makes a mistake. He leaves the case just where it was before.

2. But we believe that the outer water baptism, as well as the spiritual, at least, is here spoken of. Of course we must remember that, by a well known figure very frequent in Scripture, baptism is said to affect what it only symbolizes. (If Messrs. McKay, Witherow, etc., had borne this in mind, they would have spared their stricture on Baptist logic which is, in this case, the logic of almost the universal Church.) Paul argues that the believers of Rome are not obvious to the taunt that unconditional justification licenses sin, because believers are dead to sin. To prove that they are thus dead, he declares that in their baptism into Christ, they were baptized into his death (the symbol being said to effect what it represents.) Then to make it plain that in their baptism into Christ they were baptized into his death, he refers them to the form of their baptism—a burial—which was to show forth this very fact, and says, "therefore—for this very purpose—we are *buried* with him by baptism into death."

Besides, in v. 5, it reads, "For if we have been planted together (lit. 'grown together,' Rev. Ver. 'united') *in the likeness of his death*," etc. Here baptism is called a likeness of the Saviour's death, referring to its representation as a burial in v. 4. Now spiritual baptism cannot be a likeness of anything. This likeness must be actual and visible, and not spiritual and invisible. What then must be the form of that outward baptism which is the likeness of the Saviour's death? Can it be anything else than the burial by baptism—the immersion—of v. 4? Can sprinkling or pouring be such a likeness? Conybeare and Howson express the idea of this verse thus: "Literally *have become partakers of a vital union of the representation of his death* (in baptism). The meaning appears to be, *if we have shared the reality of his death, whereof we have undergone the likeness.*" Well may they say, then, "This passage cannot be understood unless we bear in mind that the primitive baptism was by immersion."*

3. The history of the interpretation of this passage throws much light upon its meaning.

The early Fathers, beginning with Tertullian who was born about 150 A.D., and including Basil, Cyril, Chrysostom, Gregory Nazianzen, Ambrose, John of Damascus, Theophylact, etc., all interpret this passage as referring to water baptism by immersion. And so do all modern scholars, so far as I can learn, until Moses Stuart, including such names as Luther, Zuingle, Wesley, Whitfield, Baxter, Adam Clark, Chalmers, Bloomfield, Conybeare, Meyer, and a host of others. Since M. Stuart's attempt to explain Rom. vi. 4, 5, so as not necessarily to include a reference to immersion, but few have had the hardihood to follow him. Until there was need, then, of a different interpretation to serve a controversial purpose in evading the force of the Baptist argument, no one thought of explaining this passage except as a reference to baptism as immersion, and few have done so even since. Who can fail to see the force of these facts?

4. Finally, the true symbolism helps to the true interpretation of this passage, and to the truth about the mode of baptism. Even Mr. McKay admits that baptism is to symbolize the work of regeneration in the soul, and Rom. vi. 4, 5, and Col. ii. 12 prove it. But how can we best represent that change by which old things pass away and all things become new—by which the old man is crucified, and the person becomes a new creature? By what stretch of the imagination can we see this shown forth in sprinkling or pouring? How can we fail to see it vividly and impressively portrayed in the burial in the water—death to the old—and rising out of the water—resurrection to the new? Baptism is

---

* Life and Epist. of St. Paul, p. 587.

represented again in Eph. v. 26, and Titus iii. 5, as a bath or bathing—the word used in the original referring to a bathing of the whole body. But how the whole body could be said to be bathed by baptism, if baptism were a sprinkling or a pouring, I find not; but in immersion I see such a bathing.

But on what does Mr. McKay and others depend, beyond what has already been answered, to evade the force of these passages?

1. Mr. McKay holds that in Rom. vi. 3, "Buried with him by baptism," the burial is the result of the baptism, and is not the baptism itself, and as the spade which buries is not the burial, therefore here the baptism is not the burial. He has forgotten, however, that on p. 27 he declares that Dr Dale has proved beyond a question that the baptism is not an act, but an effect; now he says, in order to serve his present purpose, that baptism is not effect, but means. He abounds in points against us. First, we are demolished because a thing is so, and then again because that very thing is not so. But whichever way he chooses to make his point, it is useless here; for if the burial is the result of the baptism, it is a burial which is the result, and that is what is always affected by immersion, and what is never secured either by sprinkling or pouring. Besides, in Col. ii. 12, it is "buried with him *in (en)* baptism, not by baptism. Therefore here it is plainly stated that the burial is the baptism.

2. It is said that the ancient burial was not a covering, but a cremation, and so the burial in water need not be a covering in water. But the Jews placed the dead in sepulchres, and of *Christian* burial, with which we have alone to do, let Smith's Dic. Christ. Ant. speak. After an exhaustive examination, it is concluded, "As a rule, accordingly, it may be held, that interment, with or without embalming, . . . obtained from the first in the Christian Churches."*

* Art. "Burial."

3. His attempt to cast odium upon what he terms the "burial theory," by declaring it Romish, will be considered in the next chapter. This declaration no one ever made who had any reputation to lose. But what shall we say of his statement, that "the best scholars during and since the Reformation have repudiated the Romish and Baptist interpretation of Rom. vi. 3-5, and Col. ii. 12? I will give a few quotations from the leading reformers and divines during and since the Reformation.

Luther: "That the minister dippeth a child into water signifieth death; that he again bringeth him out of it, signifieth life. So Paul explains Rom. vi." In Du Veil on Acts viii. 38.

Zuingle: "The immersion of your body into water was a sign that ye ought to be ingrafted into Christ and his death; that as Christ died and was buried, ye also may be dead to the flesh and the old man." Annot, Rom. vi. 3.

Presbyterian Assembly of Divines: "'Buried with him by baptism.' In this phrase the apostle seemeth to allude to the ancient manner of baptism, which was to dip the parties baptized, and, as it were, to bury them under the water, for a while, then to draw them out of it, and lift them up, to represent the burial of the old man, and our resurrection to newness of life." Annot, Rom. vi. 4.

Cranmer: "Baptism and dipping into water doth betoken that the old Adam, with all his sins and evil lusts ought to be drowned and killed by daily contrition and repentance, and that by the renewing of the Holy Ghost we ought to rise with Christ."*

John Wesley: "Buried with him—alluding to the ancient manner of baptizing by immersion."†

Thus I have quoted the words of the leaders in the German, Swiss, Scotch, Anglican, and Methodist reforma-

---

* An Instruction of Baptism. † Com. in Loco.

tions, and they all adopt the "Baptist and Romish" interpretation. Had I space I could quote from one hundred and fifty and more of the most prominent Protestants of all denominations to the same effect. I do not believe a half dozen Protestant scholars of any note can be found who will deny a reference in Rom. vi. 3-5, Col. ii. 12, to immersion. And yet Mr. McKay can declare that the best scholars during and since the Reformation have repudiated this interpretation, and that it is Romish. It is pitiable for any man to be so carried away by a desire to prejudice the minds of his readers against the view he combats, as to be guilty of such statements.

But what a somersault this new ground requires our Pedobaptist friends to make? To bring in affusion, their great argument is that the Spirit is said to be affused, and that the water baptism is to be affused also, because it must conform to the representation of the Spirit's baptism. Whereas, now, to get rid of burial by baptism, they declare that this refers to the Spirit's baptism, but that the water baptism need *not* conform to the representation of the spiritual. How convenient! If they would only notice that the effects of the Spirit on the soul, and not the mode! of the Spirit's coming is called a baptism, then there would not be this apparent conflict between the representations of the spiritual baptism, which requires them to contradict themselves point blank.

A word or two about other references to baptism. Saul is thought to have been baptized standing, because he "arose and was baptized." There are but few besides Mr. McKay who do not know that "arise" in Scripture use means to "prepare," "get ready," see Josh. i. 2, Judg. v. 12, etc. It is thought that when Peter asks, Acts x. 47, "Can any forbid water," etc., it means, can any forbid its being brought into the house. Wonderful! The baptism of the jailer is not said to be "in the jail," Acts xvi. 32-34, and if it was, it would not disprove immersion.

Thus we have followed our author through his remarks on the references to baptism in Scripture. We have been compelled to notice much which demands attention only because some thoughtless people might think it unanswerable, if unanswered, and because it is a compend of what is usually advanced, especially by unscholarly people, who venture to deny that immersion is baptism. The reader must form his own conclusions. The most convincing argument, however, if anything can be more plain than the language of Scripture, still remains.

CHAPTER VI.—THE ARGUMENT FROM HISTORY.

As Mr. McKay tells us, he began his pamphlet with the determination "to carry the war into Africa." Men more learned and hence more discreet have not ventured to do more than attempt to prove that sprinkling is valid baptism as well as immersion. Mr. McKay, however, to fulfil his valorous threats, seeks to show that immersion is not baptism. After having treated the argument from the meaning of the word *baptizo*, and from the references to baptism in the Bible, as we have seen, he proceeds to the testimony of history, and makes the astounding assertion that immersion is

A ROMISH INVENTION!!

This is the latest discovery. Common sense people will wonder how this pastor, in his retired study, with his modest shelves of books beside him, has been able to find out what Church Historians and Encyclopædists, with their life-long research among musty manuscripts, and the records of the past, never dreamed of. The most, we have no doubt, will be unkind enough to think that the Historians are as trustworthy as Mr. McKay, although he taxes such men as Schaff and Stanley with blundering, p. 112. It is hard to deal with such a statement as this seriously. I may state that I have examined the works of all the Church Historians of England, America, France and Germany. I have been able to find in the great libraries of Europe and America, and I have yet to find one who refers to the primitive baptism, who does not declare that it was by immersion. So also of the works on Archæology.

We propose to question history and the Church Historians as to the original mode of baptism, and whether immersion or sprinkling is allied with Rome.

In the Epistle of Barnabas, esteemed canonical by some in the earliest times, we find these references to baptism:—

"Blessed are they who, placing their trust in the cross, have gone down into the water." "We descend into the water full of sins, but come up, bearing fruit in our heart."

Hermas, writing about the close of John's life, describes the apostles as having gone "down into the water," with those they baptized, and "come up again."

Justin Martyr, writing about A.D. 140, speaks of the baptized as "washed," and as obtaining forgiveness of sins "in the water." He exclaims again: "For what is the benefit of that baptism which makes bright the flesh and the body only!"*

Tertullian, A.D. 204:—

"Of baptism itself there is a bodily act, that we are immersed (mergimur) in water."

"We are three times immersed (mergitamur)."

"Entering into the water, we profess the Christian faith," etc.†

In three other passages he speaks of baptism as an immersion, using the word *tingo*.

---
* Apol. 79, 85, 86. Dicl. cum Trypho. Ch. XIV. † Corona Militis, Ch. III. Baptism, Ch. VII. De Spectaculis, Ch. IV., etc.

Hippolytus, A. D. 225, speaking of our Lord's baptism:

"How was the boundless river which makes glad the city of God, bathed in a little water, the incomprehensible fountain . . . covered with scanty and transitory waters.

There is not yet the remotest hint of sprinkling or pouring as baptism. But it was about to appear. The idea began to prevail that baptism was necessary to salvation. Hence when any were sick and in danger of death, being unable to submit to immersion, they were sprinkled or poured as a substitute.

The first instance of such a baptism is the case of Novatian, A. D. 250. The following facts speak for themselves:

1. Eusebius, in his history, written less than a century after, quotes as follows from a letter of Cornelius, a bishop contemporary with Novatian: "He (Novatian) fell into a grievous distemper, and it being supposed that he would die, immediately he received baptism, if indeed it be proper to say that one like him did receive baptism." *

2. Novatian recovered, and was nominated for Bishop. In reference to this, Cornelius in his letter to Fabius, says "All the clergy, and many of the laity resisted it, since it was not lawful that one baptized in his sick bed by aspersion, as he was, should be promoted to any order in the clergy." †

3. One Magnus inquires of Cyprian the great N. African bishop of the time, "Whether they are to be esteemed right Christians who are not washed in the water, but only sprinkled (non loti sunt, sed perfusi." ‡

---

* In my reference to this passage in my review, not having Eusebius in the original at hand, I took the translation of Dr. Hiscox. The translation given above is preferable. The change does not affect the argument. A generous opponent would not use such a case as Mr. McK. does, to impute ignorance or forgery to his reviewer.

† Bohn's Eccl. Lib. ‡ Quoted by Bp. Taylor, Doct. Dubit B. 3, Ch. IV. K. 15, and Pengilly, Baptism, p. 78.

BAPTISM: AN ARGUMENT AND A REPLY. 71

4. Cyprian, with great diffidence replies, "In the sacrament of salvation (baptism), where necessity compels, and God gives permission, the divine thing, though outwardly abridged, bestows all that it implies on the faithful."*

5. People who were thus sprinkled on their beds, partly, at least, from the inadequacy of their baptism, were not permitted to hold office in the church." †

6. The Edinburg Encyclopedia gives the further history of sprinkling. "The first law to sanction aspersion as a mode of baptism was by Pope Stephen II., A. D. 753. But it was not till the year 1311 that a council held at Ravenna declared immersion or sprinkling to be indifferent," etc. ‡

One more fact need but be mentioned to make the absurdity of the assertion that *immersion* is an invention of Rome, patent. The statement, I give in the words of Dr. Wall, Hist. Inf. Bap. II. p. 414. No one but a very ignorant man can question it. It is, "All

---

* Neander, Ch. Hist. I. p. 310. † Kurtz, Ch. Hist. I. 30-1 and 45-2.

‡ Mr. McKay, referring to this quotation, says in his review, "It is unfortunate for this statement *that there was no General Council held at Ravenna in the year 1311,*—the Baptist Robinson to the contrary, notwithstanding." Now any reader of this confident and emphasized statement would suppose Mr. McKay knew. There may be some surprise when I state that Mr. McKay makes this denial without having examined the facts, or regardless of them. The Encyclopedia Brittannica, states "The Council of Ravenna in 1311 was the first council of the Church which legalized baptism by sprinkling, by leaving it to the choice of the officiating minister."

Meyer's great Encyclopedia (Das grosse Conversations Lexicon), the most learned work in Germany, says, (I translate) First, Since the 13th century, at the council of Ravenna, 1311, became aspersion (probably on medical grounds) permitted."

To be absolutely sure I consulted, in the Library of the British Museum, London, Labbé's "Sacrorum Conciliorum Collectio," (Collection of the Sacred Councils). Under the year 1311 was the Council of Ravenna, among whose acts was the one on baptism referred to by the learned authorities.

Mr. McKay retains this false statement in his later editions.

those nations of Christians that do now, or formerly did, submit to the authority of the Bishop of Rome, do ordinarily baptize their infants by sprinkling or pouring. But all other Christians in the world, who never owned the Pope's usurped power do, and ever did, dip their infants in the ordinary use."

Thus we find that sprinkling—not immersion—comes to us with the stamp of Rome upon it. Well may that most learned of German works, Brockhaus' Real Encyclopadie, Art. Baptism, say:

"The mere sprinkling with water which earlier was the practice only in the case of the sick, came into use in the Western (Roman) Church for the first in the thirteenth century. The Protestants brought this custom over from the Catholics, (nahmen diese Sitte von den Catholiken heruber)."

While sprinkling was thus early practiced in extreme cases, and we might well suppose that some early writer would refer to it as a form of baptism, yet not one single reference of the fathers of the first four centuries can be found to literal water baptism as a sprinkling. I quote a passage from each of the principal ones, who wrote in Greek.

Cyril of Jerusalem, A. D. 315. Instruction III., on Baptism, 12:

"Thou, going down into the water, and in a manner buried in the waters as he in the rock, art raised again, walking in newness of life."

Basil, A. D. 330. On the Holy Spirit, Ch. XV. 35:

"Imitating the burial of Christ by the baptism: for the bodies of those baptized are as it were buried in the water."

Chrysostom, A. D. 347. John's Gospel, Discourse XXV:

"When we sink our heads down in the water as in a kind of tomb, the old man is buried," etc.

Athanasius, about 390. Questions on Psalms, Prop. 92:

BAPTISM: AN ARGUMENT AND A REPLY. 73

"For that the child sinks down thrice in the font and comes up, this shows the death and the resurrection," etc.

Gregory Nazianzen, A. D. 330. Discourse XL:
"Let us, therefore, be buried with Christ by the baptism," etc.

These quotations might be continued for pages, but I forbear.*

It is no wonder then that ALL CHURCH HISTORIANS who have expressed themselves, Pedobaptists though they be, unanimously declare that the original baptism was immersion, and that sprinkling came in later, in case of the sick.

Let us quote a few of the greatest of them as to the practice of the first three centuries.

Neander, a prince of historians, Ch. Hist. I. p. 310:
"In respect to the form of baptism, it was in conformity with the original import of the symbol performed by immersion. . . . It was only with the sick, when the exigency required it, that any exception was made, and in this case baptism was administered by sprinkling."

Giersler, Ch. Hist. 1. p. 277:
"The condition of catechumens continued several years; but the catechumens often deferred even baptism as long as possible on account of the remission of sins by which it was to be accompanied. Hence it was often necessary to baptize the sick, *and for them the rite of sprinkling was introduced.*"

Kurtz, p. 119: "Baptism was performed by thrice

---

*Mr. McKay, Pamphlet, p. 52, evades the force of the testimonies of the primitive writers in a way which few would care to do. He calls Basil, Cyril, Chrysostom, Gregory Nazianzen, Photius, and Theophylact, *Romish* writers ! ! ! Surely a *very* poorly informed man always risks the strongest assertions. What will the reader think, when he calls to mind that these were *all* Greek Fathers of the East,—that Chrysostom was Patriarch of Constantinople, the rival of Rome, and that Photius was the leader of the Greek Church in its final separation from Rome. See Hagenbach Hist. Doc. I. p. 230. Kurtz Ch. Hist. Sec. 67. Comment is needless.

6

immersing. Sprinkling was only common in case of the sick."

Hase, German edition, ps. 111, 112: "Baptism was performed by a trine immersion, in case of the sick by sprinkling."

Schaff, probably the greatest living Presbyterian scholar, Hist. of Apost. Ch. p. 568: " Finally, as to the outward mode of administering this ordinance, immersion and not sprinkling, was unquestionably the original, normal form. This is shown by the very meaning of the Greek words *Baptizo, Baptisma, Baptismos*, used to designate the rite. Then again by the analogy of the baptism of John, which was performed *in* the Jordan, (en), Matt. iii. 6, Comp. 16, also *eis ton Jordanen*, Mark i. 9. Furthermore by the New Testament comparison of baptism with the passage through the Red Sea, 1 Cor. x. 2, with the flood, 1 Pet. iii. 21, with a bath, Eph. v. 26, Tit. iii. 5, with a burial and resurrection, Rom. vi. 4, Col. ii. 12.

Finally, by the general usage of ecclesiastical antiquity (as it is to this day in the Oriental, and also the Greeco-Russian Church), pouring and sprinking being substituted only in cases of urgent necessity, such as sickness and approaching death."

Dean Stanley, Art. Bapt.: " For the first thirteen centuries the almost unanimous practice of baptism was that of which we read in the New Testament, and which is the very meaning of the word baptize, that those who were baptized were plunged, submerged, immersed into the water. . . . Baptism by sprinkling was rejected by the whole ancient church (except in the rare case of death-beds or extreme necessity) as no baptism at all."*

---

*On the cover of Mr. McKay's pamphlet is a plate representing the King and Queen of the Longobardi (?) sitting in a bath and being poured. Hear what Mr. McKay says: " Their sitting in the water in the family bath is immersion; but their baptism is by water poured on them from a vase. Their immersion, like that of the Greek church of the present day, was far from being a *submersion* of the whole body

BAPTISM: AN ARGUMENT AND A REPLY. 75

And so, had I space, I could quote to the same effect from Cave, Gregory, Winer, Kahnis, Waddington, Smith, Mosheim, Hagenbach, Fisher. Pressensè, etc., and these are all Pedobaptists, and the most noted church historians who have ever lived. As I have not space to quote, I will challenge any one to produce a single church historian who has ventured to state that sprinkling and not immersion was the practice of the primitive church. I will also challenge an instance, in any church father of the first three centuries after Christ, who refers to literal Christian baptism with water as a sprinkling—literal Christian baptism, I say, for the early writers saw a figurative baptism in many things.

But what do the Encyclopedias testify.

I consulted all contained in the British Museum Library, London. The following is the result:

Encyclopedia Brittanica: "The usual mode of performing the ceremony was by immersion. In the case of sick persons the minister was allowed to baptize by pouring water upon the head, or by sprinkling. In the early church, clinical baptism, as it was called, was only permitted in cases of necessity; but the practice of baptism by sprinkling gradually came in, in spite of the opposition of councils and hostile decrees."

Burrow's and Wilkes' Encyclopedias and Pantologia all adopt the following statement: "In performing the

---

under water, and would not be recognized as baptism by modern immersionists. Yet it is of just such immersions that Dean Stanley speaks, whom Baptists claim as sustaining their practice." Dean Stanley says above that baptism was a submersion, and yet Mr. McKay says he did not mean immersion at all. To what lengths of wild assertion will he not go to carry his point, and the "war into Africa." Here is another passage from Dean Stanley's Eastern Church, p. 117. "There can be no question that the original form of baptism was complete immersion in the deep baptismal waters, and for at least four centuries any other form was either unknown or disregarded, except in case of dangerous illness as an exceptional almost a monstrous case. To this form the Eastern Church still rigidly adheres." By this same method he seeks to eliminate immersion from the New Testament and to substitute sprinkling.

ceremony of baptism, the usual custom (except in clinical cases, and where there was scarcity of water) was to immerse and dip the whole body."

English, Penny, and National Cyclopedias state: "The manner in which it (baptism) was performed appears to have been at first by complete immersion."

Rees' and Howard's Cyclopedias: "In primitive times this ceremony was performed by immersion, as it is to this day in the oriental churches, according to the original signification of the word."

Encyclopedia Metropolitana: "We readily admit that the literal meaning of the word baptism is immersion, and that the desire of resorting again to the most ancient practice of the church, of immersing the body, which has been expressed by many divines, is well worthy of being considered."

Edinburgh Encyclopedia: "Baptism, in the apostolic age, was performed by immersion."

London Encyclopedia: "It is certain that the literal meaning of the word baptism is immersion, which is further confirmed by the practice of the ancient church."

Chambers's Encyclopedia: "It is, however, indisputable that in the primitive church the ordinary mode of baptism was by immersion. . . But baptism was administered to the sick by sprinkling, although doubts as to the complete efficacy of this *clinic* (sick) baptism were evidently prevalent. . . . The dispute concerning the mode of baptism became one of the irreconcilable differences between the Eastern (Greek) and Western (Romish) Churches, the former generally adhering to the practice of immersion whilst the latter adopted mere pouring," etc.

I add translations of what two of the greatest German Encyclopedias say.

Meyer's Das Conversations Lexicon:

"The first mode of baptism (immersion, untertanchen) was practiced in the apostolic as well as in the primitive church, and is continued in the Eastern Church, which regards sprinkling as arrant heresy, and has made it a ground of their separation from the Western (Roman). Yet there existed a sprinkling already, at that time, in case of the sick."

Hertzog's Real Encyclopadie:

"In the primitive church we find immersion (unter-tanchen) as a rule in baptism, pouring and sprinkling being only in case of the sick."

In view of all this, and much more which might be advanced, did space permit, how absurd is the attempt of Mr. McKay's pamphlet to arouse prejudice against immersion, by branding it as Romish. How unseemly, also, are all the efforts which are made to obscure the plain facts of history, which declare that immersion, and immersion only, was the primitive baptism. Probably also, those of these most learned of the world's scholars who are alive, would smile did they hear that Rev. W. A. McKay had declared that they "knew little and cared less about 'dipping,'" p. 27. But the testimonies of all the church historians and encyclopedists must be got rid of in some way; for they are all compelled to concede that immersion is the original baptism. And so Mr. McKay sweeps them all aside by the authoritative assertion that they were all careless ignoramuses, so far as what they assert about baptism is concerned.

But Mr. McKay's attempt is worse than absurd He says, p. 57, "The very first mention of dipping as a mode of baptism is by Tertullian, who lived about the beginning of the third century." Why did he not state that sprinkling is not mentioned until half a century later, and then it is to question it ? He seems to have put it so purposely, to leave the impression that immersion was but then being introduced, and that sprinkling had been the practice up to this time. Again he seeks to discredit immersion because it was threefold until the seventeenth century. "Those who did not dip three times did not dip at all." Why did he not add also that, during the same time, those who did not sprinkle three times, did not sprinkle at all ? Such a resort to half truths which teach a lie is utterly unworthy of a Christian controversialist.*

Again, Tertullian is said to have included immersion among the observances " based on tradition, and destitute of scriptural authority." He does just the opposite. In De Corona Militis, chs. 3, 4, he mentions traditional observances associated with baptism, but he gives no hint that the immersion itself was traditional, while in other places, he expressly declares that baptism was by immersion, and by our Lord's command. These are his words: " As of baptism itself there is a bodily act, that we are immersed (mergimur) in water," etc. De Bap. ch. 7. " And last of all, commanding that they should immerse (tinguerunt) into the Father and the Son and the Holy Spirit." Against Praxeas ch. 26.†

In his absurd attempt to fasten upon immersion the odium of being Romish, Mr. McKay meets with a grave difficulty. The Romish church to-day practises sprinkling, and Pedobaptists, and not Baptists, are at one with Rome in reference to the form of baptism. How then

---

* Mr. McKay, in reply to my statement that it was as much the custom, until the 17th century, to sprinkle three times as to immerse as usual flatly contradicts it. Of this, he says, "*there is no proof whatever,*" p. 103. A denial is needed, and he makes it. But what are the facts. The American Cyclopedia, Art. Bap., declares "The Latin Church favors affusion three times."

Meyer's German Conversations Lexicon declares that sprinkling, permitted by the Council of Ravenna, "has certainly gone over into the Protestant church as a threefold one."

Richard and Gerand's Bibliotheque Secreè, French, Art. Bap. "They (Christians) immerse (the candidate) three times, or they cast water on his head three times (on lui verse trois fois de l'eau sur la téte)."

Dr. Wall, Hist. Inf. Bap. I. p. 576, gives acts from the Synod's of Angiers and of Langres, from the Council of Cologne, and from the Agenda of the Church of Mentzs instructing the Priest to sprinkle three times And so the proof might be multiplied, were it needed.

(Mr. McKay, in his last edition, has corrected this blunder. We oenretain the criticism because it is independent interest.)

† Mr. McKay, p. 106, waxes both merry and indignant at my translating *tinguerunt* in this passage, immerse, and he asserts, as usual, as

BAPTISM: AN ARGUMENT AND A REPLY. 79

can immersion be Romish, while sprinkling is Rome's practice?

Here is Mr. McKay's solution: "During the twelfth and thirteenth centuries the Church of Rome was compelled by the force of the example of the Presbyterian (!) Waldenses to abandon her superstitious dipping and return to the simple and Scriptural baptism by affusion," p. 116.

Now, as every school boy knows, the Church of Rome was bending every energy, during the most of this time, to sweep the Waldenses from the earth with fire and sword, and every divergence from Romish beliefs and practices was visited with death. And yet Mr. McKay has the hardihood to assert that Rome actually was forced by the example of those whom she was hounding to the death, to change her form of baptism! The fact is that the Waldenses did not baptize, but left the baptism of their children to the priests of Rome (See Herzog Hist. of Waldenses), and there is not a shred of evidence or any statements of Church Historians for any such assertion. It is the purest fiction of Mr. McKay's brain.

He also says, p. 58, that the Waldenses put dipping as among the superstitions of Rome, and refers to Perrin, Ch. III. p. 231. I can find no such statement there.

though he was certain, that this verb "*never means immerse*," p. 104. Any tyro in Latin, especially ecclesiastical Latin, should know better. His own Dr. Dale gives *tingo* but two meanings, to dip, and to die, making it the exact equivalent of the Greek *bapto*. In the Lexicons of Adams, Forcellinus, and Riddle's Scheller, dip is given as the primary meaning of *tingo*, while Ainsworth, under tinctus, gives dip as its *ecclesiastical usage*. Smith's Christian Antiquities refer to this very passage where *tingo* is used of baptism, to prove that triple *immersion* was the rule in North Africa, where Turtullian lived. Art. Bap. sec. 49. The translators of the Ante Nicene Library translate (tinguimur) in the last of this same passage "immerse." Ed. Beecher, Congregationalist, declares "Tertullian uses *tingo* interchangeably with *mergo, mergito* (to immerse)." Christ Rev. 1849, p. 241, and "But to prove that it means immerse is needless; no one can deny it." And so I might quote from M. Stuart, Prof. Toy, Prof. Tobey, Dr. Hovey, &c. So much for this proof of Prof. Goodspeed's ignorance and unfairness. There is quite a number of just such instances.

Elsewhere Perrin states, "The things which are not necessary to baptism are . . . dipping it (candidate) thrice in water." Thus they admit a single immersion to be baptism, but object to the threefold dipping. There is no proof that they had any other objection.

Mr. McKay even attempts to make it appear that the learned Church Historians and Encyclopædias have all "blundered," in stating that immersion has always been the practice of the Greek Church. Of course, this is absurd to even a tyro in ecclesiastical history. As evidence to confound all the learned authorities, he refers to the statement of one Huber and of a correspondent of the New York *Independent*. For the benefit of the unlearned reader, I give extracts from the authoritative Confessions of Faith of the Greek Church, as found in Schaff's "Creeds of Christendom." In "The Orthodox Confession of the Eastern (Greek) Church," in answer to question 111, baptism is defined as "a triune immersion in water." In "The Larger Catechism of the Russian Church"—the chief modern representative of the Eastern or Greek—in answer to question 288, baptism is declared to be "a sacrament in which a man who believes, having his body thrice plunged in water," etc. In answer to question 290, "What is most essential in the administration of baptism?" it is replied, "Triune immersion in water."

I add the testimony of a few more of the learned authorities. Schaff's can be seen in a foot note. Schaff adds, "The Oriental and the orthodox Russian churches even require a threefold immersion, and deny the validity of any other."

Herzog's Encyclopædia:—

"The practice of sprinkling first came into common use at the end of the thirteenth century, and was favored by the growing rarity of adult baptism. It is the present practice of the Roman Church; but in the Greek Church immersion is insisted on as essential."

Edinburgh Encyclopædia:—

"The Greek Church universally adheres to immersion."

Encyclopædia Americana:—

"The Greek Church retained the custom of immersing the whole body, but the Western (Roman) adopted, in the thirteenth century, the mode of baptism by sprinkling."

The reader can now better judge who has "blundered."

He also states, p. 115, that putting the whole body under water is not necessary to Greek baptism, and adds, that he "can produce records of Greek baptism as old as the fifth century, where the priest is forbidden to allow the head of the child to go under the water," and then has the audacity to declare, "This is the kind of immersion that John Calvin said was practised by the ancient (not apostolic) church, and this is the kind of immersion that all the eminent scholars since the Reformation have found in the writings of the Greeks and Roman Catholics." Whether John Calvin did not refer to apostolic baptism as an immersion, and a complete immersion, can be best understood from his comment on John iii. 23:—
"From these words, John iii. 23, it may be inferred that baptism was administered by John and Christ by plunging the whole body under water."

He does not refer the reader to the records he speaks of. If they do not have reference to exceptional cases where the ordinary immersion gives place to sprinkling because of the weakness of the child, the records have not yet met the eyes of church historians and scholars, and he had better produce them by all means. This attempt, on the ground of these mysterious records, to make the testimony of the scholarship of the world in favor of immersion of none effect, will not have the weight of a feather with any upon whose ignorance and credulity he is not able to rely to the utmost. I can only challenge him to produce the slightest shred of evidence that any of the scholars who declare that immersion was the ordinary practice of the ancient church, referred to partial immersion. The reader can turn to the quotations elsewhere and judge for himself.

The reader of Mr. McKay's pamphlet will notice that he does not give any quotation favorable to sprinkling from any of the apostolic and early Fathers of the church. The reason is, that there is no reference in their writings to the act of baptism as a sprinkling; the scores and scores of references to it are always as an immersion. We hope the force of this fact will be weighed by the unprejudiced reader.

NOTE.—What Mr. McKay has not done, Mr. Lathern, Baptisma, p. 146, sq., has attempted, in a pretended reference to Patristic Testimony. He gives no hint that there are scores of plain and express declarations, in the writings of the early Fathers, that baptism was an immersion. But he refers to some figurative allusions to baptism, which, out of their connection, seem to favor affusion, and leaves it to be inferred that this is all the evidence from the Fathers, and that it is against immersion. How much even the figurative allusions he quotes favor sprinkling, can be seen when the passages are given. I shall give what Mr. Lathern quotes in ordinary type, and add the part of the passage which he omits, in italics, and leave the reader to judge for himself.

Cyril, of Alexandria, Com. on Isaiah, Ch. iv. 4:—

"We have been baptized not with mere water, nor yet with the ashes of a heifer *have we been sprinkled, errantismetha,* but with the Holy Spirit and fire."

Chrysostom, Homily II.:

"Wonder not that I call martyrdom a baptism, for there also the Spirit descends in rich abundance, . . . *and as they who are baptized are bathed with the waters, so are the martyrs with their own blood.*"

Tertullian, Baptisma, 16. Translation 3, Ante Nicene Library:—

"These two baptisms He shed forth from the wound of his pierced side, *in order that they who believed in his blood might be bathed with the water, they who had been bathed in the water might drink of the blood. This is the baptism which stands in lieu of the fontal bathings.*"

Gregory Nazienzen, Orat. xxxix. 17: "I know a fifth, the baptism of tears, *but it is still more difficult, because it is necessary to wet one's couch every night with tears.*" "*But*," he explains, Orat. lx. 9, "*how many tears have we to shed before they equal the flood of the baptismal bath?*" See Hag. Hist. Doc. I. p. 358.

Mr. Lathern assumes, p. 201: "Where Tertullian follows the law of Scripture, he spoke of aspersion of water in baptism," and refers to the expression *periginem aquæ*, "sprinkling of water." De Penitentia 6, for proof.

I give the passage in which this expression occurs, as translated in the Library of the Fathers, from which the reader can judge of this proof. Here it is: "For who will furnish to thee a man so unfaithfully repenting, a single sprinkling of any water?" Tertullian challenges any one to find such a case. Immediately after he speaks of baptism as a "washing" in a "laver."

The reference by Origen to I Kings xviii. 33, expreses strongly his idea of the completeness of the drenching, as though it had been an immersion. As Mr. Lathern scarcely ever tells us where to find his quotations, I cannot identify the other three, but presume the connection would explain the expressions as in the cases given above. They are but figurative allusions at best, teaching nothing about the act of water baptism. When these same writers refer to this, it is always as an immersion.

The attempt to make it appear that Tertullian admits immersion to be a tradition, without Scriptural authority, p. 200, may impose on the unlearned, but it will provoke a smile from others. Suffice it to say, that no church historian agrees with Mr. Lathern. The expression, "Dehinc ter mergitamur amplius aliquid respondentes, quam Dominus in Evangelio determinavit," Mr. Lathern declares is Tertullian's frank confession "that the practice of triune *immersion* was 'more than the Lord prescribed in the Gospel.'" How correct this construction is, can be judged from the translation of the whole sentence, which I give: "Then we are thrice immersed, answering somewhat more than the Lord prescribed in the Gospel." It was the custom to catechise the candidate while standing in the water. Tertullian says that the "responses" thus required were not commanded. So Smith's Christ. Ant. explains these words of Tertullian: "He speaks then of other 'responses' made by the baptized while standing in the water, alleging these as an example of custom founded on tradition only, not on any express direction of our Lord."* So also Neander,† etc

I have not space to refer at length to Mr. Lathern's remarks on the testimony of the fonts. He is most unfortunate, however, in alluding, p. 154, to that Ephesian font (?) discovered by Mr. Wood, fifteen feet in diameter and nine inches deep. Why such an immense vessel should be needed to sprinkle candidates for baptism does not appear. Then it was found in the Forum, and not in a Church. Did Christians baptize in the Forum? It is similar to a vessel found in a heathen temple. It was found within the territory of the Greek Church, where immersion has been always the practice. This chimera of Mr. Wood, at least, will not "hand his name and fame to posterity." The smallest of the fonts which Dr. Robinson says, Lex. Art. *Baptizo*, were too small for immersion, is, according to his own measurement, Bib. Res. I. p. 78, four feet in diameter on the outside, and three feet nine inches deep. When the reader remembers these fonts were not erected until infant baptism became general, he will see the absurdity of assuming that they were for sprinkling infants. They are very large for immersing them. Indeed, Dr. Hackett who examined them, declares them fully large enough for adult immersion.

Mr. Lathern refers to the evidence as to the mode of baptism in the Catacombs at Rome, and quotes Witherow. The facts are found in Smith's Dic. Christ. Ant., the most

---

* Art. Bap. sec. 10. † Ch., Hist. I. p. 308.

learned work in the language on this and kindred subjects. Speaking of the only baptistery known to exist in the Catacombs—that in the cemetery of St. Pontianus, it says: "This consists of a small cistern or 'piscina,' supplied by a current of water. This piscina would appear to be between three and four feet deep and about six feet across."* It is added, "It is perhaps one of the earliest examples now remaining of a chamber set apart for the performance of this rite" (baptism).

Mr. Lathern, p. 156, remarks: "An elaborate effort has been made by the able but erratic Robinson, in his 'History of Baptism,' to obtain evidence from the practice of the early pure ages in favor of immersion. According to his own acknowledgment, 'there were no baptisteries within the churches till the *sixth century.*'"

This statement is made to make it appear that Robinson could find no evidence for immersion, until this late period, from baptisteries, because no baptisteries existed previously. If this is not the purpose, why use this "acknowledgment" of Robinson? Robinson declares there were no baptisteries *within the churches* till the sixth century, because prior to that time *they were a separate building.* These are his words:—

"About the middle of the third century baptisteries began to be built; but there were none within the churches till the sixth century; and it is remarkable that though there were many churches in one city, yet (with a few exceptions), there was but one baptistery." p. 69.

In the Art. Baptistery in Smith's Dic. Christ. Ant., reference is made to many baptisteries before the sixth century. To explain why they were in separate buildings, he refers to the fact that baptism "in the earlier centuries" being by immersion, the receptacles for the water were too large to be conveniently placed in churches. This can be readily understood when we are informed that this receptacle in the baptistery of the Lateran, the most an-

---

* Art. Baptistery.

cient of those existing, was twenty-five feet in diameter, and three feet deep, and in that of Sta. Maria Maggiore twenty feet across by five feet deep.

The Encyclopædia Britannica gives the reason why Robinson "acknowledges" there "were no baptisteries within the churches till the sixth century":—

> "In the ancient church it was one of the buildings distinct from the church itself. Thus it continued till the sixth century, when the baptisteries began to be taken into the church porch, and afterward into the church itself."*

Kurtz gives the reason for bringing the baptisteries into the churches, thus:—

> "When infant baptism became general, separate baptisteries were no longer necessary, and instead of them, stone *fonts* were placed in the churches."†

Other points in "Baptisma" might be discussed, had we space or inclination. But we have neither.

Chapter VII.—Summary.

Thus we have striven to meet objections to immersion fairly. The reader must judge whether they have not been met sufficiently—nay, whether the most have not proved arguments for us, scarcely disguised. In every case but one or two, we have referred the readers to the passages of the author where our quotations may be found, so that they can verify for themselves. In the course of the discussion, also, the following facts, among others, have been made apparent.

On the assumption that immersion was the baptism practised by Christ and the apostles, all is clear and consistent.

The Greek word *baptizo* is taken in the sense in

---

* Art. Baptism. † Ch. Hist. I. p. 237.

BAPTISM: AN ARGUMENT AND A REPLY. 87

which the people used and understood it—in the sense in which the Greeks of to-day, and the church of which they form a part, use and understand it—instead of having forced upon it a meaning not only totally foreign to it, but also that of another common word in the language, thus doubly confusing and misleading the people. The references to baptism in the New Testament are simple and easily understood, requiring no departure from the ordinary use of language. 'In' is not required to be changed to 'at,' 'with,' etc., nor "into" to 'to,' etc., nor 'out of' to 'from.' Neither do we have to advocate the strange idea of a washing or bathing of the whole body by sprinkling a few drops of water on the face, nor are we required to say that the application of these drops is a burial, as baptism is declared to be. As would be expected on the supposition that the baptism of the apostles was an immersion, we find the writers of the first and second and succeeding centuries declare it to be such, and when sprinkling and pouring are introduced we find them regarded as only permitted as baptism when immersion could not be administered, and even in this case they were regarded as insufficient to qualify for offices in the church, while sprinkling only gained an equality with immersion through the Pope of Rome, by whom also the Virgin Mary is put upon an equality with the Son of God, and this only after thirteen centuries.

On the supposition, however, that sprinkling was the baptism of the New Testament we have to face the following absurdities:

1. Our Lord chose the word in Greek which always meant to immerse and never to sprinkle, to designate the act of sprinkling, instead of taking the word *rantizo* which ever meant to sprinkle. Thus our Lord made it necessary for all who spoke of the Christian ordinance to explain that *baptizo* in reference to it, did not mean *baptizo* but *rantizo*, and whenever there was no one to

make this explanation, the people were most surely deluded.

2. In the New Testament references to baptism, in addition to unnatural uses of prepositions, etc., and fanciful explanations of the need of much water for sprinkling a few drops upon each candidate, we must understand the apostles to describe such sprinkling as a bathing of the whole body, Eph. v. 16, Titus iii. 5, a washing of the whole body, Acts xx. 19, Heb. x. 22, a burial, Rom vi. 4, Col. ii. 12.

3. Although our Lord commanded sprinkling, and the apostles practiced it, Barnabas and Hermes, who were contemporary with the latter, refer to baptism in terms only consistent with immersion, and Justin Martyr, who wrote within forty years of John, and all the earlier fathers, in scores of references to baptisms, always describe it as an immersion, which it was not, and never speak of it as a sprinkling, which it always was, in apostolic times!

4. Nay more, if sprinkling was the practice of the apostles, then within one hundred and thirty or two hundred years after their time so absolutely had the knowledge of the practice faded from the mind of the church, that when the original baptism by sprinkling was again administered, two hundred and fifty years from the birth of Christ, all the church looked upon it as to be allowed only when immersion was impossible, and even then as so inferior to immersion that those who had been sprinkled were disqualified for church offices! Will Pedobaptists please explain how within such a short period the practice of the apostles could have been abandoned in the whole church, and not only abandoned but entirely forgotten. What led the church to wish the change? As the change took place and was forgotten in the space of three generations, what made the change so sudden and general? How did it happen

that no grandfather ever told of the old baptism to his grandchildren or no grandchild ever remembered it?

In view, then, of the fact that all lines of evidence agree in requiring immersion, and that all lines agree in rejecting sprinkling and pouring, so that the assumption that the apostles ever practiced it is attended by such absurdities as the above, the reader can judge whether Mr. McKay's challenge to Baptists to produce a single undoubted instance of immersion from the Bible, needs any further attention.

Neither let the reader suppose that the only question between us and other denominations, as to the mode of baptism, is merely one of more or less water. The real issue is on a principle which has to do with adherence to all truth. It is this, shall we feel ourselves bound to yield an exact obedience to the definite instructions of our Lord, thus avowing our belief that he had a specific purpose to serve in the ordinance as he commanded it, which cannot be so well served in any other way; or shall we take the liberty to change what he has ordained, thus encouraging a spirit of looseness and rashness, while we attribute to our Lord the folly of enjoining what is so immaterial that so distant an approach as sprinkling is to immersion will do as well as that which He commands. The nature of the issue can be seen in the words of John Calvin, Institutes IV., XIX., " But whether the person who is baptized be wholly immersed, and whether thrice or once, or whether water be only poured or sprinkled upon him, is of no importance. Churches ought to be left at liberty in this respect to act according to the difference of countries. *The very word baptize, however, signifies to immerse, and it is certain that immersion was the practice of the ancient church.*" Baptists, on the contrary, hold that the form of baptism is adapted by divine wisdom to serve the divine purpose, and that therefore neither John Calvin nor any one else can tamper with it, or enjoin a different form, without putting himself in opposition to Christ.

Finally, may we not urge upon the reader the duty of giving to this question a calm and unbiassed consideration? To be on the side of truth in all things is to be on the side of God in everything; for He is Truth. To be on the side of error in anything is to be against Him in something. We shall soon all be in our graves, and any saving of self denial through wilfully or carelessly remaining in partial error, will not serve us. But the man who has been willing to suffer even that God's truth in its wholeness may have the devotion of his life shall then have eternal honor.

PART II.

THE SUBJECTS OF BAPTISM.

CHAPTER I.—INFANTS EXCLUDED FROM THE BAPTISM OF THE NEW TESTAMENT.

In considering the question of the proper subjects of baptism, I shall not so much review any Pedobaptist writer, as state some of the reasons why Baptists reject infant baptism and the arguments used in its support. I shall, however, correct some of the mis-statements of Mr. McKay and others.

1. Our first proposition is:—

Infants are excluded from baptism by every description of this rite. 1. Infants were excluded from *John's Baptism.* This was the "baptism of repentance," Mk. 1:5; Acts 19:4, viz.: in token of repentance. In harmony with this, the candidates were exhorted to "bring forth fruits meet for repentance," Lu. 3:8, and were "baptized" confessing their sins, Matt. 3:6; Mk. 1:5. As infants cannot repent and confess sin, they were shut out from John's baptism.

2. Infants were excluded from *the baptism of our Lord, during his life.* John 4:1 declares "Jesus made and baptized more disciples than John." According to this, the only description of this baptism, our Lord made people disciples before he baptized them. As to make disciples means to lead to faith on Christ by instruction, —infants which can neither be taught nor believe, were excluded from this baptism.

We need not discuss the question whether this baptism was the same as that enjoined in the Commission. It is evident that in the baptism of John and of our

Lord, the only baptisms of which the apostles knew, when the Commission was given, infants were excluded. Unless, therefore, infants were expressly included in the Commission, they would have continued their previous practice, and have omitted their baptism. But it requires only candid reading of Matt. xxviii. 19; Mark xvi. 16, to be convinced that

3. *Infants are excluded from the baptism enjoined by the Commission.* As some may object to Mark xvi. 16, because wanting in full MS. authority, let us confine our study to the Commission as given by Matt. xxviii. 19. This reads in the Revised Version: " Go ye, therefore, and make disciples of all the nations, baptizing them in the name of the Father, and of the Son, and of the Holy Ghost, teaching them to observe all things whatsoever I command you," etc. Now to make disciples of Christ, in the New Testament sense, is always to lead to faith through instruction. The command then is to lead all the nations to faith in Christ through preaching the gospel, baptizing those thus led to Christ, etc. As infants are incapable of being led to faith by instruction, they are excluded from baptism by the terms of the Commission.

Some Pedobaptists, however (see McKay, p. 73, Lathern, p. 101), attempt to include infant baptism in the Commission by virtually making it read: " Make disciples, etc., by baptizing," etc.* But this is adding to the Scripture. It also fails to note the fact just stated, that " make disciples " is to make believers through instruction, which baptism does not do for any. Besides, in the desire to include infants in the Commission, our Pedobaptist brethren seem blind to the fact that they thus

---

* Mr. McKay states that " this is the view of the Commission taken by nearly all the best commentators," p. 73. This is another of his assertions made at a venture. Ingham quotes from between one and two hundred of the most noted commentators and scholars, all Pedobaptists, who speak of the Commission as applying to adults only. (See Subjects of Bap. 21 sq.)

exclude adults. For adults are not, by their own belief, to be made disciples by baptism and succeeding instruction, but to become disciples as prerequisite to baptism.* Neither do any believe that the apostles so practised. Indeed, this was impossible, for men would not have submitted to baptism prior to instruction and faith on Christ. But the Commission as thus explained, will not include even infants, for infants are not thought to be made disciples by Pedobaptists by baptism and teaching " to observe whatsoever I (Christ) have commanded you" (disciples), but by baptism and believing, which the apostles were not commanded to do, being believers already. It is best, therefore, to take the Commission as it reads, otherwise confusion and contradiction result. Thus we see the natural Scriptural order is, Disciple, Baptize, teach Christian observances

None but adults, then, can be the subjects of the baptism of the Commission. This Commission, also, was given for all time. But if our Pedobaptist friends accomplish their aim, the time will come when none but infants shall be baptized, and the only baptism consistent with its terms will cease to be practised. Need I ask whether that practice can be true which would thus, at some time, make altogether void the command of Matt. xxviii. 19, which was to hold through all time?†

But if, as we have found, the apostles knew no infant

---

* Mr. McKay, in his characteristic way, p. 62, asserts that Baptists often "speak and write as if they alone maintained adult or believer's baptism," and terms this "exceedingly dishonest." I know of no Baptist who has stated that Pedobaptists would not baptize an adult believer. He should name one who has been guilty of this folly, if he knows a case.

† Both Mr. McKay and Mr. Lathern seek to make it appear that the Baptist argument from Mark xvi. 16, against infant baptism, would damn infants. Our argument, in the form of a syllogism, is this. No baptism but that of believers is taught in the Bible. Infants cannot believe. Therefore infants are not to be baptized. Now if Mr. McKay or Mr. Lathern will show us that there is no salvation in the Bible, but that of believers, as there is no baptism, then we will say also, because infants cannot believe, they cannot be saved. But we believe there is

baptism before our Lord gave them this last command, and as this command excludes infant baptism, then we must suppose they did not practise it. If we find on examination that they did not baptize infants, this will be another link in the chain of conclusive evidence. This leads us to our next remark.

4. *Infant Baptism was excluded in apostolic practice.* Let us refer to every case mentioned in the New Testament.

At Pentecost, only such as "gladly received the word" were baptized, Acts ii. 41, not these and their children.

The Samaritans believed, and "were baptized, both men and women," Acts viii. 12. Now we cannot doubt but that there were children belonging to some of the multitude baptized. Had such children been baptized, is it not as nearly certain as can be that the record would have mentioned the fact, and would have read, "were baptized, men and women, and children"? If infants of believing parents were baptized in *any* case, they were in every case. As they were not at Samaria, we believe they never were.

There were no infants baptized in the baptism of the household of Cornelius, Acts x. 46, 47; for those baptized had received the Holy Ghost, and spake with other tongues.

There were no infants in the household of the Jailer: for Paul spake the word to all that were in the house, and they all shared in his faith, Acts xvi. 32, 34.

---

a salvation other than through faith. So we believe infants can be saved, while they are not to be baptized.

Mr. Lathern, p. 98, quietly assumes that Baptists do not "cherish solicitude in regard to the dedication of infants to God," because they do not baptize them. Is it necessary to say that Baptists are showing as much concern for their children as any others? But they do not think the submission of an unconscious babe to a mechanical rite, has anything to do with the well-being of the child. One prayer of the parent, and one act of faith by the babe when come to years of understanding, are better in our estimation, than all forms which do not exercise the moral nature.

There were no infants in the household of Crispus: for they all believed with him, Acts xviii. 8.

There were no infants in the household of Stephanus, I Cor. i. 16, for in less than five years after their baptism they had already "addicted themselves to the ministry of the saints," I Cor. xvi. 15, and the Corinthians were exhorted to be subject to them.

There were no infants among those baptized at Corinth; for they all hearing, believed, and were baptized, Acts xviii. 8.

The only remaining instance of baptism apart from the case of Simon, Acts viii. 13, and of the Eunuch, Acts viii. 36 sq., which require no notice, is that of Lydia's household, Acts xvi. 15. All the probabilities are against an infant being there. She was probably unmarried, as it was not the custom of the East for married women to do business in their own name. If she were married, it is most improbable that she would take young children with her on a business journey to a distant city, such as she was making. The household were probably the servants who assisted her in her business. Besides, we find there were brethren in Lydia's house a few days after the baptism of the household, to whom Paul bade adieu at his departure, Acts xvi. 40. These brethren must have been the baptized household, as we have no evidence that there were other converts. Under such circumstances, we are not required to assume that this household was different from the rest baptized.*

---

* Mr. McK. takes our translators to task again for translating *oikos* household, and not family, and adds, "Were it not for this blunder on the part of our translators, together with the 'into' the 'out of,' and tne 'much water,' the Baptist denomination never could have existed." Now, should the world accept Rev. W. A. McKay at his own estimate, it would go hard with the Baptists. But when people know that the learned authors of the Revised Version retain "household" as the translation of *oikos*, as they do the other "blundering translations," they may think there is a possible hope for the Baptists still.

In his last edition, he does not venture longer to retain this charge about the translation of the word *oikos* "household." It is not more

A general remark about the baptisms of households. Our Pedobaptist brethren do not seem to see that household baptisms cannot prove anything for infant baptism, without proving too much.

They assume that the household was baptized as a matter of course, on the faith of its head, and speak of the improbability of all being converted. Very well, let the household be baptized on the faith of its head, then, and what follows? There must have been the wife and servants and grown-up children, or at least some of them, in every household. Then, to justify infant baptism, through assuming that infants were baptized on the faith of the head of the house, we make it necessary to baptize the adult unbelieving members of any household whose head has believed. Let our Pedobaptist friends cling to infant baptism if they will, because of household baptism, but let them be consistent, and hold also, that adult unbelievers have a right to baptism, when members of a household whose head has believed.

5. *Infants are most definitely excluded from baptism by its significance.* In Rom. 6: 3-5, all who were baptized are said to have signified, in their baptism, a vital union with Christ, by which they die to sin and rise to newness of life. But have infants been brought into a new relation to Christ? If they are vitally united

---

absurd, however, than many which remain. He says, however, p. 77, that *oikos*, the word translated household, "means family, and has special reference to little children." He quotes Taylor as giving fifty examples where *oikos* has the sense of family. Now, anyone can see that to prove *oikos* to mean family does not establish what Mr. McKay states and needs to prove—that it "*has special reference to little children,*" for in almost all families there are more of responsible age than of those who are not. This word and *oikia*, which he seeks to distinguish from it, both mean, primarily, "house," and secondarily "those who dwell in a house," whether young or old, or domestics. Of course his stroke at Baptists on the charge that they both affirm and deny, as occasion calls, that *oikos*, "household," includes children, is like very many others. The charge is entirely untrue. We hold that it neither necessarily includes nor excludes children, in its meaning; but that in the households mentioned in connection with baptism, the accompanying accounts show that they included none who did not believe.

to him, have they ever been separated from him? If they are in a state of spiritual life, have they already passed over into it from a state of spiritual death? To such as were baptized in infancy Paul's argument would have been an absurdity.

So also in Col. 2 : 12, "Having been buried with him in baptism, wherein ye were also raised with him through faith in the working of God, who raised him from the dead. And you being dead through your trespasses and the uncircumcision of your flesh—you, I say, did he quicken together with him." Revised Version. Infants have no faith which all the baptized are here said to have. Neither have they been quickened from a state of death through trespass, to one of life. So infants were excluded from the baptism administered at both Colosse and Rome. But if there was no infant baptism at Colosse and Rome, there was none anywhere; for we cannot suppose there was one rule for one place and another for another.

Baptism is also to signify the complete purification which attends the death to sin and resurrection to newness of life—regeneration. Hence Paul was commanded to "be baptised and wash away his sins," Acts 22 : 16. The Hebrew saints were to have their hearts sprinkled from an evil conscience, and their bodies washed with pure water—baptized—Heb. 10 : 22. But can baptism signify purification to babes—*purification*; mark—not purity. If they are pure, have they been previously unclean, and been purged, so that baptism can thus signify cleansing? Only one reply is possible.

6. *Infants are also excluded from baptism by its purpose.* Gal 3 : 27, declares that all "who have been baptized into Christ, have put on Christ." I do not know of any who deny that baptism is here said to be a profession of faith in Christ. So evident is this that in the case of the infant, sponsors have been appointed to make this profession on its behalf. Because it is a pro-

fession of faith, it came in the New Testament immediately after believing. But can infants have faith to profess? This purpose of baptism cannot be served in their case.

In I. Peter 3: 21, baptism is called "the answer (interrogation R. V.) of a good conscience toward God." This can but mean that in each case where baptism is according to Scripture, the baptized acts according to a good conscience. But unconscious babes can have no conscience, good or bad, in anything. As this purpose of baptism is without limitation to church or age, it excludes infant baptism absolutely and forever.

Thus we have found that infants were excluded from the terms of John's baptism, of that of our Lord while on earth, of the Commission, and from the practice of the apostles. The evident reason for this exclusion has also been found in the fact that baptism, in case of the infant, could signify nothing it was intended to symbolize, and serve no purpose for which it was designed.

What shall we say then? Had infant baptism been the practice along with adult, can we suppose the New Testament would have been without mention of a case? Had infant baptism been the usage, can we conceive there would not have been at least one single description of its design and purpose which would include infants. Can an outward rite, which was not commanded or practiced by our Lord and his apostles, and which serves none of the divinely appointed purposes and designs of baptism, be recognized as valid baptism? Can we suppose our Lord intended such a rite as this to become the substitute of the one which fulfils all the purpose and design of baptism as described and practiced in the New Testament? Nay, are we to suppose it was his desire that, by the gradual progress of the gospel, pedobaptism was to become universal, and thus the time come when the descriptions of baptism in the New Testament should be no more fulfilled in any case of baptism and thus lose all meaning to men? Let such as can, believe this, I cannot.

But upon what supposed Scripture proof do our Pedobaptist friends rely to justify infant baptism in the face of these undeniable facts.

Matt. 19 : 14, "Suffer the little children to come unto me, and forbid them not; for of such is the kingdom of heaven," is appealed to. Some aver that "of such" here, does not mean, of such an humble spirit, and declare that children are prepared for heaven without the purging out of the bias to sin in the nature. But concede they are pure, and need no change, and it does not make them fit subjects for the baptism of the New Testament. They have never, then, been anything else than pure. But the baptism of the New Testament is a washing to symbolize purification, Acts 22 : 16, not purity,—it is a burial and resurrection to symbolize a new spiritual birth, a life which has succeeded a death in sin, not a life which has been from the first. Besides, baptism to them can never be the answer of a good conscience, and a profession of faith. So even though infants were pure, baptism to them could serve none of the purposes which Scripture declares must be served in all cases of baptism.

Another passage is quoted, I Cor. vii. 14: "For the unbelieving husband is sanctified in the wife, and the unbelieving wife is sanctified in the brother (husband): else were your children unclean, but now are they holy."

Unless driven to desperation for some New Testament ground for their practice, Pedobaptists would never appeal to this passage. Let us very briefly examine it.

First: It shows supreme ignorance of the history of the exegesis of this verse to say, as Mr. McKay does, that *Baptists* translate it, "'Else were your children bastards' in the height of their desperation," etc. These are the facts. Pedobaptist scholars quite generally so interpret it, including John Calvin, Beza, Doddridge, Whitby, Barnes, Bloomfield, Erasmus, Wolf, Bengel, Newcombe, Cranmer, Camerarius, Melancthon, Musculus, etc., while Dr. Gill, so far as I can find, is the only Baptist who takes this view of the passage.

Second: Notice, the same holiness is asserted of the brother (husband), as of the child. As this holiness, whatever it be, *does not* entitle the unbelieving parent to baptism, Pedobaptists themselves being witnesses, how can they assert that this very holiness does entitle the child to baptism?

Third: The apostle is speaking *of* the cases of mixed marriage *to* the believers at Corinth. Hence the expression, "else were *you* children unclean," must refer to the children of the believers to whom he addressed his epistle. The apostle, then, assumes that the unbelieving wife or husband is as holy as the children of believers. So Olshausen, De Wette, Meyer, Dressler, Bengel, etc.

Fourth: Now if the children of believers had been baptized, either because of their purity or for any other reason, they would have had the same standing as their believing parents, instead of being compared to the unbelieving husband or wife in these mixed marriages. This passage thus so plainly shows that infants were not baptized in apostolic times, that Wiberg, the great Swedish Baptist, was first led by its study to distrust the scripturalness of infant baptism, and such Pedobaptist scholars as Dean Stanley, Stier, Lutz, Neander, Lange, Meyer, DeWette, Ruckert, Muller, etc, concur in the statement of Olshausen: "It is evident that Paul would not have chosen this way of arguing, if infant baptism, already, at that time, had been in use."

The adducing of Acts ii. 39, "The promise is unto you and your children"* as proof of infant baptism,

---

* Mr. Lathern, Baptisma, makes this one of his chief—the chief—argument for infant baptism. Now there cannot be the shade of a doubt that children here means descendants. If it meant "the promise is to you and your infants, it would shut out all but the infants of that generation. But allowing that children here, means descendants, and what imaginable bearing it can have on infant baptism, I fail to see. It says, virtually, that the promise of salvation is for all the generations to come. The consistency of some of our Pedobaptist friends adding, "therefore, infants are to be baptized," is not very apparent.

needs no serious reply : for children here is in the sense of descendants, as any can see who chooses to read the connection. Neither does the assertion that children are in the church, on the evidence of II John i.; I John ii. 13 ; Eph. vi. 1-3 ; Col. i. 2, meaning by children—infants. Let the reader turn to these passages, and there will be need of no word from me.

Eph. ii. 19, 20, " Ye are fellow citizens with the saints, and of the household of God ; and are built upon the foundation of the apostles and prophets," etc., is termed, " Baptisma," p. 91, " Paul's authoritative and masterly statement on the subject" of "the identity of the Church of God through all dispensations." Now to justify infant baptism, it is not enough to show that there was a church of God in the Old Testament—the Jewish nation, into which infants were born, must be that church. To serve Mr. Lathern's argument, the "saints" here with which the Ephesian believers were made fellow citizens, must have been the members of the Jewish nation, against whom Paul had shaken off the dust of his feet as incorrigibly opposed to Christ. Mr. Lathern will scarcely attempt to maintain this. "The foundation of the apostles and prophets" has been variously interpreted. Some think it means the gospel as taught by the New and Old Testament, others, as taught by the apostles and prophets (teachers) of the New alone. Others still, the foundation on which apostles and prophets rested for salvation. But however interpreted, there is no shadow of ground for the use made of it by Mr. Lathern. Alford says, "saints" here is the mystical body of Christ, the commonwealth of the spiritual Israel. Besides, Paul addresses the Ephesians, who are thus made fellow citizens with these saints, as having been quickened from the death in trespasses and sins, etc., Eph. ii. 1 sq. The saints, then, with whom they thus became fellow citizens, must have possessed spiritual life, and could not have been a body of people, introduced by a mechanical rite into the church of God, and growing up, a large share of them at least, in ungodliness. But enough.

The breaking off the wild olive branches (Israel as an unbelieving nation), and the grafting in of the believing Gentiles, Rom. 11: 18-20, is taken by Mr. McKay, p. 71, as a proof that the church of God of the New Dispensation is the same essentially as the church of God of the Old. Who denies this? Certainly God had a people among the Jews, but these did not include all the nation, and men were not members by natural birth, but by spiritual. So Paul says, Rom. 9: 6, "For they are not all Israel (spiritual) who are of Israel (natural)." For this very reason, because the natural and national Israel were unbelieving, they were broken off from the old believing patriarchal stem, and the believing of the Gentiles grafted in. Now pedobaptism seeks to do what Paul declares God had overthrown, viz.: give men a place in the visible kingdom of God—the church—by natural birth. Paul says God broke off the Jewish nation from the believing patriarchal stock because of unbelief. Pedobaptism says, let all be grafted in by natural birth, growing up in unbelief, as they surely will, until they are led to faith. Thus pedobaptism, to justify itself, seeks to restore the old Jewish national idea, which was set aside in Christ. Is it any wonder then that the practice which requires us to set aside the spirituality of the new dispensation, and go back to the vanished principle of Judaism, meets with the most determined opposition from Baptists?

Thus we find that there is no design or purpose of baptism which can be served in case of unconscious babes. They were not baptized in apostolic practice. Neither is there a passage or allusion in the New Testament which favors infant baptism—nay, which is reconcilable with it. Need I ask, in view of all this, can infant baptism be authorized or valid?

Chapter II. Alleged Old Testament Evidence.

Strange as it may appear, Pedobaptists depend chiefly on the Old Testament for support of this assumed New Testament ordinance of infant baptism. Their first argument is this:—

1. The church of the Old Testament and that of the New are essentially identical. Infants were included in the former, therefore they must be in the latter, and be subjects of its initiatory rite-baptism.

Let it be distinctly understood that what our Pedobaptist friends mean by the church of the Old Testament is the nation of Israel. This is not denied, and alone will help the Pedobaptist argument. This is explicitly asserted by Dr. Hodge, vol. iii, p. 558, "God made a nation his Church and his Church a nation." The Israel to which infants belonged by right of descent from Abraham was the Jewish nation. They did not belong to any spiritual Israel, including those only of the nation of Israel who were the real servants of Jehovah. This was not entered under the Old Economy any more than under the New by natural birth. Under both the condition of membership was the new birth. Let there be no confusion here. What Pedobaptist writers mean by the Old Testament Church is the nation of Israel. If they do not mean this, they have no ground of argument for their practice from the Old Testament. They must and do assume that the Jewish nation and the New Testament Church are essentially identical.

The chief alleged proof of this identity is Acts 7: 38, where the Israelites are called the Church in the Wilderness. In quoting this as proof it is assumed that the word *ecclesia* is never used except of the Church of God. Then in Acts 19: 22, the Ephesian mob, which cried "Great is Diana of the Ephesians," must have been essentially a Church of Christ: for they are termed an *ecclesia* as well. The truth is, this word means "assembly" generally, and is used where there is no reference to a church. Thus it is in this case. Acts 7: 38. The apostle, following the general practice of the Seventy, uses *ecclesia* as the translation of the Hebrew *Rahal*, assembly or congregation.*

But if the Israelites in the wilderness did constitute, essentially, the Church of God in the New Testament sense, then what a constitution a Church of Christ may have!

In Acts 7: 39, these Israelites are described as disobedient and idolatrous. In Heb. 3: 7-19, we learn that through their sin and unbelief they were shut out from Canaan, and died in the wilderness. If then these were the Church of God, to which the New Testament Church is to conform, then a Church of Christ may be composed of such as are shut out of heaven through unbelief and sin. If it be necessary, in order to support infant baptism, to plead for such a constituted church, then may the Lord deliver us from it.

But what is the constitution of a New Testament Church?

Paul addresses or speaks of the members of the churches at Jerusalem (Acts 9: 13), Lydda (Acts 9: 32), Rome (Rom. 1: 7), Corinth (Cor. 1: 2), Ephesus (Eph. 1: 1), Philippi (Phil. 1: 1), Colosse (Col. 1: 2), as *saints*.

He addresses the churches at Rome, Thessalonica and Galatia as brethren (Rom. 12: 1, I Thess. 1: 4, Gal. 1: 11). He calls the members of the church of Thessalonica "holy" (I Thess. 5: 27), of the Hebrew churches "holy brethren" (Heb. 3: 1).

---

* Mr. McKay tells his unlearned readers, p. 65-69, etc., that God's ancient people are called an *ecclesia* (church) in various Old Testament passages, as though the Old Testament scriptures were written in Greek and not in Hebrew. He is of course quoting from the translation of the Seventy, where *ecclesia* is used in the ordinary classical sense of assembly or congregation. Our translators, in view of the special New Testament meaning of *ecclesia* (church), have not translated a single Old Testament passage where *Rahal* (congregation or assembly) occurs, by the word church, thus showing that they did not think that the old congregation of Israel was essentially a church, in the New Testament sense.

The church at Corinth is called "the temple of God which is holy" (I Cor. iii. 17), and it is exhorted to be separate from unbelievers (II Cor. vi. 14-16). The church at Ephesus is called the "body of Christ" (Eph. i. 22 sq.), "an habitation of God in the Spirit" (Eph. ii. 22). To the members of the church at Colosse Christ had imparted life and forgiveness (Col. ii. 13).

And so we might enlarge to almost any length.

Now can any one, on sober thought, maintain that these descriptions could apply to the Jewish nation, which was as sinful as it well could be?

But notice further. If all are to be received into the church by right of natural birth, as all became members of the Jewish nation, then, as in the new dispensation, the whole world are on an equality, all men are born in the church and have a right to baptism in recognition of this fact. Let pedobaptism, then, gain what it seeks, and all infants will be baptized, and grow up in the church, thus obliterating all distinction between the church and the world. Can this be the idea of the grand consummation which the Scripture writers had in view? Do they not contrast the church and the world in all their references to the two? One is light, the other darkness. One is holy, the other corrupt. One is subject to Christ, the other to Satan. And yet the theory to justify infant baptism is such that it requires the progress of the gospel gradually to make these one, not by changing the first into the last, but by including the world in the church, through bringing all into her in infancy, to grow up in her, and make her corrupt with the reeking corruption of innate depravity and sin. So, to make it appear that that is baptism which does not meet any of the New Testament descriptions, apostolic administration, design, and purpose, we are asked to assent to an argument which makes equally empty all the New Testament descriptions of a church of Christ. There is at least consistency between the practice to be upheld and the argument to sustain it.

How simple, however, is the matter when we are willing to take plain New Testament teaching.

Instead of the New Testament church being like a nation, into which men are born, the kingdom of heaven is spiritual and not national, and men are to become members not by natural birth, but by spiritual regeneration, John iii. 1.

So Paul does not say to the Jews, you belong to the kingdom of heaven—to the church of Christ—by natural birth. This is the very idea he had to combat. The Jews supposed they had membership in the Messianic kingdom, even as in the national realm, by virtue of natural descent from Abraham. But Paul tells them, in relation to the spiritual dispensation of Christ, that they that are of faith are children of Abraham, Gal. iii. 7. This argument for infant baptism, viz.: that the Jewish nation and the Christian church are essentially the same, is just the position of the Judaizers of old, who misunderstood the spiritual nature of the new dispensation. Can any wonder that we cannot consent to have infant baptism forced upon the New Testament by such an argument as this? Can we do less than protest against a practice which destroys the constitution of the Church of Christ, and opens it to bad and good alike?

2. It is said that the Old Covenant and the New are essentially one. Infants received the seal of the Old —circumcision. Therefore they should receive that of the New—baptism.

Let us test this statement.

It is said, Heb. viii. 8 sq., "Behold the days come, saith the Lord, when I will make a new covenant with the house of Israel and with the house of Judah; *not according* to the covenant that I made with their fathers in the day when I took them by the hand to lead them out of the land of Egypt," etc., and in v. 13, "In that he saith a new covenant, he hath made the first old. Now that which decayeth and waxeth old is ready to vanish away."

The argument for infant baptism from the covenants requires that the new be according to the old, which flatly contradicts Scripture which declares that the new is *not* according to the old.

So Gal. 4: 22 sq. Here Paul compares the two covenants to the bond-woman Hagar, and the free-woman Sarah. The old he says "from mount Sinai, beareth children unto bondage, which is Hagar." But Jerusalem that is above and is free, is the mother of the free children of the new. The argument from the covenants to support infant baptism requires us to suppose that the contrasts between the bond-woman and the free, the children born to slavery, and to freedom, Mount Sinai, and the Jerusalem which is above, here made, are descriptions of what is essentially the same. And so we could point to the whole scope of the New Testament, and show that the old and new covenants ever stand in contrast to each other.

I will give an outline of the argument, which the reader can fill out for himself.

1. The Old Covenant of Circumcision and the New Covenant of Grace were not for the same classes.

That of Circumcision was for the natural seed of Abraham and their slaves, Gen. xvii. 10-14. It was a race covenant, a national one.

That of Grace was for a spiritual seed, John iii. 3-7, etc., which is ever opposed by the natural, Gal. iv. 28, 29. That of Grace was for the children of Abraham through like faith, Gal. iii. 7-9, 25-29.*

2. The benefits of the two are not the same.

---

* Mr. Lathern actually quotes Gal. iii. 27-29, to support the idea that in the New Covenant as in the Old, blessings descended to the natural seed. Has he read the preceding verses, where faith and not baptism is spoken of as the condition of sonship and blessing? Has he read v. 7, "They that be of faith, the same are sons of Abraham," and v. 9, "They which be of faith are blessed with faithful Abraham"? How then can he hold that the blessings of the Covenant of Grace are for the natural seed, and not the spiritual through faith?

That of Circumcision did not include salvation, Gen. xvii. 1-14.

That of Grace is saving, Heb. viii. 6-13.

3. They were not the same in their condition.

That of Circumcision was circumcision, Gen. xvii. 10-14.

That of Grace is faith, Rom. iv. 16, etc.

4. They are contrasted in their relation to the law.

That of Circumcision included the law, or was included in it, Gal. iv. 21 sq.; v. 1 sq.; John vii. 22, 23; Acts xxi. 20, 21; Rom. ii. 25, etc.

That of Grace excluded the law, or was excluded by it, Rom. vi. 14, 15; xi. 6; Gal. v. 4, etc.

I quote one passage, Gal. v. 1-4: "Stand fast, therefore, and be not entangled again with the yoke of bondage. Behold, I, Paul, say unto you that if ye receive circumcision, Christ will profit you nothing. Yea, I testify again to every man that receiveth circumcision, that he is a debtor to do the whole law. Ye are severed from Christ, ye who would be justified by the law, ye are fallen away from grace." (Rev. Ver.)

Paul says that such as are circumcised put themselves under the law, and are thus out of the realm of grace, and severed from Christ. And yet, to get an argument for infant baptism, we are told that baptism takes the place of circumcision as the seal of a covenant essentially the same as that of circumcision. If this be so, then it follows that all the baptized are severed from Christ, etc.

How much more simple to accept the plain declarations of Scripture, and believe that the Old Covenant, being national, all were, by national birth, entitled to its blessings; while the New, being spiritual, none but those who have spiritual birth—regeneration—have a right to its benefits, and to its sign.

Another form of this argument is this:—

Baptism was substituted in place of circumcision

Infants were circumcised. Therefore infants should be baptized.

1. But if baptism takes the place of circumcision, it must have the same *adult* as well as infant subjects. But adult slaves were to be circumcised, with no regard to moral character, Gen. xvii. 12, 13, while no adult is to be baptized unless a believer on Christ, Acts ii. 41, etc. So also in Gilgal, Josh. chap. v., all the Israelites were circumcised, bad and good. Can we say, then, that baptism must take the place of circumcision in case of the infant, when we know it did not, in case of the adult? This would be argument with a vengeance.

2. If baptism takes the place of circumcision, they must have the same infant subjects. But they have not. Circumcision was for males only. Baptism was for both sexes.

3. If baptism takes the place of circumcision, the apostles would not have practised both together. But they did, Acts xvi. 3.

4. If baptism took the place of circumcision, Paul would have mentioned it. The Judaizers were ever persecuting him because they thought he set aside circumcision. If baptism was virtually circumcision in another form, would he not have silenced their outcry by telling them so? But how different was the course of the apostles. Judaizers are teaching the Gentile converts that they must be circumcised, Acts xv. The apostles and brethren meet to consult. Peter asks, v. 10, "Why tempt ye God, to put a yoke upon the neck of the disciples, which neither our fathers nor we were able to bear?"

They conclude, Acts xxi. 25, that the Gentiles are to observe "*no such thing.*" Yet to have support for infant baptism, we are told that baptism is just such a thing as circumcision, which placed this unbearable yoke on the Jews. Either the apostles or the Pedobaptist friends who use this argument must be wrong.

But let us hear the gist of Mr. McKay's argument for baptism as the substitute of circumcision.

"The inspired apostle," says he, "tells us that 'Abraham received the *sign* of circumcision, a *seal* of the righteousness of the faith which he had while he was uncircumcised' (Rom. iv. 11). Here then circumcision was a *sign*. Like baptism, it represented the circumcision of the heart, or regeneration. For the real 'circumcision,' says Paul again, 'is of the heart, in the spirit, and not in the letter, whose praise is not of men but of God' (Rom. ii. 29). It was also, like baptism, a seal. It testified to 'the righteousness of the faith which he had,' and to his acceptance of the conditions of that everlasting covenant in which Jehovah Jesus said to him, 'I will be a God to thee and thy seed after thee.'

"Baptism and circumcision are, therefore, of the same general import, both being divine appointed *signs* and *seals* of the same great covenant promises and obligations, and of the same great truth of the necessity of the Spirit's work upon the soul. The Apostle Paul speaks of baptism being substituted for circumcision,— 'Beware,' he says, 'of the concision; for we'—we who have been baptized—'are the circumcision, who worship God in the spirit' (Phil. iii. 2, 3). Again, 'Ye are circumcised with the circumcision made without hands, in putting off the body of the sins of the flesh by the Christian circumcision, buried with Him in baptism' (Col. ii. 11, 12). In other words, those who are baptized have what Paul in this passage calls Christian circumcision."

All we need say in reference to this exposition of Rom. iv. 11. is this. If circumcision was a sign of "regeneration" to Abraham: if as a seal it testified to the righteousness of the faith which he had, and to his "acceptance of the conditions," etc., its purpose as thus described in Abraham's case was special to him; for when given to adults, Gen. xvii. 12, 13; Josh. chap. v. it had no reference to moral character, much less regeneration or the righteousness of faith, and in the case of infants, there was no regeneration or faith or acceptance of a covenant to signify or seal. One has but to read Rom. iv. 11 sq., to see that the purpose specified by the apostle in Rom. iv. 11, was really a special one to Abraham, in a spiritual sense, as the father of all that believe, whether circumcised or uncircumcised, Jew or Gentile. It is most misleading to take this description of a special use of circumcision, in a single case, to establish a general identity of purpose of circumcision and baptism, and, from this, to assume that the general purpose of circumcision which is not embodied in this special case, must have its counterpart in baptism and infants be included in its subjects. Even in Abraham's case, the apostle says nothing about circumcision "testifying to his acceptance of the conditions," etc., and of its being a sign and seal "of covenant promises and obligations," and of "the necessity of the Spirit's work upon the soul." Paul says of Abraham, that the sign of circumcision was a seal of a righteousness of faith already had, not of a promise to give it on conditions, or of a Spirit's work yet to come. Now, taking Paul's words and not those of Mr. McKay, and restrict circumcision, in his individual case, to a seal of the "righteousness of faith," if baptism is to serve the same purpose, then, in case of the infant, it must seal the righteousness of another's faith and not its own to the baptized, and we have baptismal regeneration as the outcome of this argument for infant baptism. But if baptism is to be the substitute for circumcision because it serves the same *general* purpose, then, because circumcision had no moral significance in the case of adults; but all the adult members of a household, including servants, were to be circumcised with the head of the house, our Pedobaptist friends, to be consistent with this argument from circumcision, as well as from their interpretation of household baptisms, must baptize all the adult members of every household whose head has believed.

So far as Rom. ii. 29; Phil. iii. 2, 3, and Col. ii. 11, 12, are concerned, it need only be said that the real New Testament and spiritual circumcision is here contrasted with the Old Testament ritual circumcision. The latter was the *type* of the former, just as the sacrifices were a type of Christ. The fact that the two are thus contrasted, proves that the outward circumcision was not given as a *sign* of the inward circumcision of the heart. We have only to refer to circumcision as described in the Old Testament, to know that circumcision of heart was not necessary before it was administered. If it did signify this, then all who were of natural descent from Abraham, through Isaac, and all their slaves and servants, were circumcised in heart by virtue of natural birth and a place in the family of an Israelite. Baptism is a *sign* of that circumcision of heart, of which circumcision was merely a type. As a sign of circumcision of heart, unless this comes through birth rather than the new birth, it cannot be given to infants, and the passages Mr. McKay uses to favor infant baptism are absolutely inconsistent with the practice.

I cannot conclude this part of the subject better than in the words of Moses Stuart, the great Congregationalist.

"How unwary, too, are many excellent men, in contending for infant baptism on the ground of the Jewish analogy of circumcision? Are females not proper subjects of baptism? And again, are a man's slaves to be baptized because he is? Is there no difference between engrafting into a politico ecclesiastical community, and into one of which it is said, that it is not of this world? In short, numberless difficulties present themselves in our way as soon as we begin to argue in such a manner as this."*

Thus we have presented the New Testament evidence,

---

* Old Test. Can.

and considered as exhaustively as space would permit, the arguments from the Old Testament by which it is sought to justify a practice as though of the New Testament, which is shut out by every New Testament reference to it.

I will add a few concessions by Pedobaptist scholars out of scores which might be quoted, and leave this part of the argument to the candid reader.

Luther: "It cannot be proved by the sacred Scriptures that infant baptism was established by Christ."*

Jacobi: "Infant baptism was established by neither Christ nor his apostles."†

Hagenbach: "The passages from Scripture cited in favor of infant baptism as a usage of the primitive church are doubtful and prove nothing."‡

Neander: "Baptism was administered at first only to adults, as men were accustomed to conceive baptism and faith as strictly connected. We have all reason for not deriving infant baptism from apostolic institution."§

M. Stuart: "Commands, or plain and certain examples in the New Testament relative to it, I find not."‖

Bp. Taylor: "All that either he (Christ) or his apostles said of it, requires such previous dispositions to baptism, of which infants are not capable, and these are faith and repentance."¶

Dr. Paley: "At the time the Scriptures were written, none were baptized but converts."**

Prof. Hahn: "Baptism according to its original design can be given only to adults, who are capable of true knowledge, repentance and faith."††

Almost any number of testimonies could be quoted from the foremost Pedobaptists, but we forbear. Of course they all have some way, tradition, church authority, continued usage, etc., to justify their practice to

---
*In A. R's Variety of Infant Bap. Part II, p. 8. †Kitto Ency. Art. Bap. ‡His. Doc. I, p. 200. §Ch. His. I, 311. ‖Bap. 101. ¶Lib. of Prof. 340. **Ser. on 2 Pet. 3:15, 16. ††Theol. p. 556.

themselves. It is significant, however, that it is not by the direct teaching of Scripture.

One general remark may be made in closing this part of the discussion. It is utterly impossible to conceive that baptism can serve the same purpose in the case of the infant and of the adult, unless it is held either that infants are born regenerate or that baptism regenerates: for it is undeniable that baptism is to signify the new birth in case of people who are responsible. It is also perfectly plain, from the teaching of the New Testament, that the Scripture writers believed that baptism served in all cases the same purpose and had the same significance. The great majority of those who hold to infant baptism take the latter horn of the dilemma, and declare, substantially, if not explicitly, that baptism effects in the infant the regeneration it signifies. This is the teaching of the symbols of the Romish, the Greek, the Lutheran and the Episcopalian churches. The Methodists are being pressed to take the other horn of the dilemma, and many of them are declaring that infants are in the same regenerate state as adult believers. This may do for brethren who believe in "falling from grace," although it threatens great damage to the whole Christian system, as might be shown, had we space. It is in vain, however, for Calvinists like the Presbyterians to hold that infants are born regenerate as the ground of their baptism; for they believe that the grace of regeneration is never lost. This would mean that the children of one or both believing parents who are to be baptized by right of natural birth are assured the new birth which makes them sure of heaven. This glaring inconsistency of the significance and purpose of infant and adult baptism must remain unsolved in their case. Neither have we seen any attempt to give Scripture proof that there were symbolisms in baptism corresponding to the different conditions of infant and adult. We commend these considerations to the attention of any Pedobaptists into whose hands these pages may fall.

Chapter III.—The Testimony of History.

About the references to baptism in the writings earlier than Justin Martyr, it may be said that they are fanciful, for the most part, and give no hint that it was for infants.

Justin Martyr was in his youth contemporary with the apostle John. He wrote an apology for the Christians to the Emperor Antonius Pius, about fifty years after John's death. In this he gives a detailed account of baptism, stating as his reason for so doing the fear lest, if he omitted to do so, he should "seem to deal in some respects perversely" in his account. He then proceeds:

"As many as are persuaded and believe that the things taught by us are true, and promise to live by them, are directed first to pray, and ask of God, with fasting, the forgiveness of their former sins; we praying and fasting together with them. Afterwards they are conducted by us to a place where there is water, and after the same way of regeneration whereby we were ourselves regenerated, they are regenerated. For they are washed in water." . . .

"And now in reference to this thing (baptism) we have learned from the apostles this reason: Since at our birth we were born without our own knowledge or choice, by our parents coming together. . . in order that we may not remain the children of necessity and ignorance, but may become the children of choice and knowledge . . there is pronounced over him who chooses to be born again, and has repented of his sins, the name of the Father. . . And this washing is called illumination, because they who learn these things are illuminated in their understanding."

If infant baptism had been the practice in Justin's day, it would have been just what he said baptism was not, viz., a matter of ignorance and necessity; and it would not have been what he said baptism always was, viz., a matter of choice and knowledge. Neither could it have been called "illumination," because those who received it were "illuminated in their understanding."

Besides, would Justin, had infant baptism been practised, have dared to promise to give an exact account of baptism to the emperor on the pretence that he feared to omit it lest he be thought to deal perversely, and then suppress all reference to infant baptism? Yet this is just what he did, was infant baptism practised in his day. If this was then the usage, Justin deliberately attempted to deceive the emperor, when deception would serve no purpose, if it were possible, and when it was impossible, if it would serve a purpose. Well, therefore, may it be said by the learned

Semisch: "Of an infant baptism he (Justin) knows nothing."

Olshausen: "In the most ancient periods, belief in Christ was indispensable to baptism, as passages from J. Martyr prove."

Semler: "From Justin Martyr's description of baptism we learn that it was administered only to adults."

Clement of Alexandria, who wrote the last of the second century, makes the following references to baptism:

"When we were regenerated (baptized) we immediately obtained the complete knowledge for which we were striving."

"This transaction (baptism) is also called grace illumination, projection, and bathing—bathing, because by it our sins are washed away; grace, because by it the guilt of our transgression is remitted; illumination, because by means of it we behold that holy saving light.'
"The bonds of ignorance are quickly severed (in baptism) by human faith and by divine grace." "Illumination is the changing of the character so that it be not the same as before baptism."

"Religious instruction leads us to faith, and faith is taught by the Holy Spirit in connection with baptism."

"Our sins being removed by one healing remedy, baptism, received in the exercise of the mind."

The idea that infant baptism was the practice, and that a large part of Clement's hearers had been baptized in infancy, is utterly inconceivable in view of the above quotations. He assumes that all the baptized among his readers had by baptism obtained knowledge for which they had been striving, had received remission of transgressions, had exercised faith, had been instructed, had had a change of character, had been baptized in the due exercise of the mind.. Who can say that infants, in baptism, could fulfil any, much less all, of these conditions? Besides, Clement is arguing with the Gnostics, and is proving the position that everything pertaining to Christianity is done in the full exercise of intelligence, and instances baptism. Now if Christians quite generally had been baptized as unconscious babes, baptism, instead of being an instance of an act done in the exercise of intelligence, would have been an instance of the exact opposite, and for Clement to use this as an instance to illustrate the general principle that all acts pertaining to Christianity are done intelligibly, would have been idiotic. So we conclude with many scholars, Pedobaptists as well as Baptists, that Clement knew nothing of infant baptism as the recognized practice of the church.

The foundation for infant baptism, however, was now laid in the idea of its necessity to salvation, which already had begun to prevail. So infants were baptized because it was feared they could not otherwise be saved.* In Tertullian's time an approach to it began to be practiced, as we learn by his opposition to it. Tertullian says: "Let them (children) come for baptism when they are growing up, when they are instructed whither it is they come; let them be made Christians when they can know Christ; let them know how to desire his salvation."†

---

* See my Baptist Principles, pp. 26, 29.   † De Baptismo, Ch. XVIII.

That this opposition of Tertullian to infant baptism, proves that it was not then regarded as an apostolic institution, is evident.

Neander says:

"Towards the close of the second century Tertullian appears as a zealous opposer of infant baptism—a proof that the practice has not yet come to be regarded as an apostolic institution; for otherwise he would hardly have ventured to express himself so strongly against it."*

It is also more than doubtful whether Tertullian had any reference to infant baptism. It is probable that he speaks of the first step toward it, since he uses the word *parvuli* and not *infantes*.

Dr. Bunsen, the learned author of "Hippolytus and His Age," says:

"Tertullian's opposition is to the baptism of young growing children; he does not say a word about new born infants."†

Hippolytus lived during the first half of the third century. Dr. Bunsen believes he would have spoken as follows to people of this century:

"We never defended the baptism of children, which in our day had only begun to be practiced in some regions." "Baptism of infants we did not know."‡

About the middle of the third century infant baptism proper had made its appearance in North Africa, as the question of Fidus, whether the infant should be baptized as soon as born, or when eight days old, proves. But this very question proves also that the practice had but just been introduced; for who can imagine such an absurdity, had infant baptism always been practiced, as that it would still be left in doubt, after over two hundred years, what was the proper age to baptize a babe, so that a council of sixty-six bishops should need

---

*Ch. Hist. I. p.p. 312.   †Christ. & Mank. II. 115.   ‡Hip. & His. Age I. p. 184.

to gravely consider a reply. The reply of Cyprian, the president, also proves the same. He, in his decision, makes no reference to the apostles and the usage of the Church,* which he undoubtedly would have done, had infant baptism been always practiced. The time of baptism, whether the eighth or the first day, was undetermined, showing conclusively that the practice was a recent innovation.

There is another proof that infant baptism was only just beginning to spread in the third century, and did not become the general practice until much later. The fathers Gregory Nazienzen, Basil, Chrysostom, and Jerome, were all born of pious parents, and yet were not baptized until manhood, while of all the forty-four or forty-five fathers of the third and fourth centuries, not one can be shown to have been baptized in infancy. Could this possibly have been had infant baptism always been practiced.†

In view of the evidence from history thus imperfectly sketched, we can see why church historians should testify as they do. We quote:

Neander: "Baptism was administered at first only to adults, as men were accustomed to conceive baptism and faith as strictly connected. We have all reason for not deriving infant baptism from apostolic institution."‡

Gieseler: "The baptism of infants did not become universal till after the time of Augustine."§

Hagenbach: "Infant baptism had not come into general use before the time of Tertullian." "In the time of Cyprian it became more general in the African church."‖

Kurtz: "After the general introduction of infant baptism the strict distinction between the "massa catechumenorum" and the "massa fidelium cease."¶ See also p. 70.

---

*Epist. 59.   †Christ. Rev. Vol. XIII. p. 218.   ‡Ch. Hist. I. p. 311.
§Ch. Hist. II. 48.   ‖Hist. Doct. I. p. 198.   ¶Ch. Hist. p. 229.

Dr. Kitto: "Pedobaptism was unknown in the post apostolic church, till Cyprian first established it as a principle. Baptism of *children* had only begun to be practiced in some countries, being defended in the time of Tertullian and Hippolytus as an innovation; but infant baptism was not known."*

Meyer: "The baptism of the children of Christians, of which there is no trace to be found in the New Testament, is not to be regarded as an apostolic institution, since it met with early and long continued opposition. But it is an institution of the church, which gradually arose after the apostles' time, in connection with the unfolding of dogmatic teaching. . . . It first became general since Augustine."†

Hase: "The necessity of infant baptism, which Origen considered an apostolical tradition, is incapable of certain proof from the New Testament. It first became general after Augustine."‡

But we forbear quoting further testimonies which might be extended to almost any length. Let it be remembered that these from whom I quote, stand in the highest rank of the world's scholars. I might, therefore, say nothing about the evidence for infant baptism which some suppose they find in a passage or two of the fathers, since these men have formed their conclusions with the most thorough knowledge of all the facts. But I will add a brief examination of these supposed patristic proofs of infant baptism which Mr. McKay and Mr. Lathern mention.

Justin Martyr speaks of "numbers of men and women . . . discipled to Christ in childhood, who still continue uncorrupt." But childhood is not necessarily infancy. Many are brought to Christ in childhood. The fact that those spoken of continued pure

---

*Jour. Sac. Sit., Jan., 1853. † Com. Acts 16 : 15. ‡Hutterus Redivivus, sec. 122.

proves that they were really converted, and so were not infants. Besides to "disciple to Christ" is to lead to personal subjection to Christ by instruction. Well may the learned Semisch say "The traces of it (infant baptism) which some persons believe they have detected in his (Justin's) writings are groundless fancies, artificially produced.* The real testimony of Justin on the subject of baptism in his day has been seen.

Irenaeus says: "Christ came to save all persons by himself—all, I say, who are by Him regenerated to God—infants, and little ones, and children, the young and the old."

But in its connection, Hagenbach, the learned church historian, declares, "It only expresses the beautiful idea that Jesus was Redeemer *in* every stage of life, but it does not say that He redeemed children *by the water of baptism*."†

Origen states that infant baptism was an apostolic tradition. But they already referred exorcism, unction giving salt and milk and honey to the baptized, and crowning him with evergreen, to apostolic tradition. Well, therefore, does Neander, the great church historian, say, "Origen declares it (infant baptism) an *apostolic tradition;* an expression which cannot be regarded as of much weight in this (Origen's) age, when the inclination was so strong to trace every institution, which was considered of special importance, to the apostles, and when so many walls of separation, hindering the freedom of prospect, had already been set up between this and the apostolic age."‡

Augustine is the only father who calls infant baptism an apostolic tradition. But Augustine calls infant communion also an apostolic tradition, which all now reject as such.

---

* Life, &c., of Justin Martyr, II. p, 334.   † Hist. Doct. I. p. 200.
‡ Ch. Hist. Vol. I.

Augustine also declares it was practiced always, everywhere and by all. Yet at the Council of Carthage, 418, at which Augustine was present, it was declared, "Whoever denies that children just born are to be baptized, let him be accursed." Jerome and Julian, two contemporaries, state that there were those who refused baptism to children, and Julian wrote against those "who supposed baptism not needful to children." The explanation is this. In Augustine's time, those who did not agree with the decisions of the general church were refused a place in it, and called heretics. As Augustine speaks of the practice in the church, the dissent of these was not noticed.

Pelagius is made to say, "I never heard of any, not even the most impious heretic, who denied baptism to infants." In view of the above facts he must have been a very poorly informed man did he say this. But he did not. His language, correctly translated, is, "Men slander me as if I denied the sacrament of baptism to infants. . . . Never did I hear even any impious heretic, who would say what I have mentioned about infants."

He was not only free from the charge of denying the propriety of infant baptism; he had so strictly abstained from all association with those who opposed this practice, that he had never heard one of them state their views on the subject.

I have finished this attempt to defend and advance truth, and commit it to the hands of Him for whose service it is meant. If any word has been written in a wrong spirit, may it be forgiven. And may the gracious Master condescend to use it in some small way.

Note.—It is matter for rejoicing that in America, where the Baptist denomination is strongest, and where its protest against

Pedobaptism is not nullified by open communion, infant baptism is rapidly dying out. In an article, a few years ago, published in the "Baptist Review," Mr. Velder shows that, by the published statistics of the various denominations, there had been the following decline in the baptism of infants, in the previous fifty years. The ratio of infant baptisms to communicants has decreased in that time—

Episcopalians	from one in	7	to one in	11
Reformed Dutch	"	" 12	"	20
Presbyterians	"	" 15	"	33
Methodists	"	" 22	"	29
Congregationalists	"	" 50	"	75

www.ingramcontent.com/pod-product-compliance
Lightning Source LLC
Chambersburg PA
CBHW031348160426
43196CB00007B/770